"This is the strategic playbook for today's l[...]
power of story to inspire and lead greatly."

> —David Morey, vice chairman o[...]
> award-winning author of *The Underdog Advantage*

"Thanks to Jim for an indispensable resource for leaders who aim to make a lasting impact with their words."

> —Dana Rubin, director of New York Speechwriter's Roundtable

"When I picked up the book, I looked first for stories of CEOs I know or feel I know. The stories ring true, as does Jim's expert advice on putting the stories to use."

> —Frank Ovaitt, president and CEO of Institute for Public Relations

"Executives who know how to tell effective business stories will influence audiences, motivate employees, and get good media attention. All executives need to master this communication skill. The wisest of executives will turn to this book to learn how."

> —Joan Detz, author of *How to Write and Give a Speech*

"This book is a must for anyone who writes or delivers speeches. Jim's techniques bring results that are instant and dramatic."

> —Virgil Scudder, CEO speech coach of Virgil Scudder & Associates Inc.

"*The Power of Storytelling* is fresh, entertaining, and, most of all, useful. The anecdotes in this book demonstrate *how* stories can best be told—but at the same time they also provide quick, powerful lessons in management, leadership, motivation, and human nature that can be put to practical use in any organization."

> —William M. Murray, president and COO of
> Public Relations Society of America (PRSA)

continued . . .

"Holtje understands that telling a good tale means delivering the satisfaction of authenticity and nothing builds more productive and more enduring business relationships than authenticity. This book is not only a little vault of anecdotal business gems, but also an arsenal of high-powered narrative artillery that every savvy businessperson should command. The book is a pleasure and a revelation."

—Jack Griffin, author of *How to Say It at Work*, *How to Say It for First-Time Managers*, and *How to Say It: Be Indispensable at Work*

"Bravo, Jim Holtje, for reminding data-driven CEOs and communications professionals that a personal anecdote, a fable, a parable, or a case history well told is always more humanizing and powerfully persuasive than an eye-glazing recitation of facts."

—Michael Morley, former president of Edelman International, adjunct professor at NYU School of Continuing Professional Studies, and author of *The Global Corporate Brand Book*

THE POWER OF STORYTELLING

Captivate, Convince, or Convert
Any Business Audience
Using Stories from Top CEOs

JIM HOLTJE

Prentice Hall Press

PRENTICE HALL PRESS
Published by the Penguin Group
Penguin Group (USA) Inc.
375 Hudson Street, New York, New York 10014, USA
Penguin Group (Canada), 90 Eglinton Avenue East, Suite 700, Toronto, Ontario M4P 2Y3, Canada
(a division of Pearson Penguin Canada Inc.)
Penguin Books Ltd., 80 Strand, London WC2R 0RL, England
Penguin Group Ireland, 25 St. Stephen's Green, Dublin 2, Ireland (a division of Penguin Books Ltd.)
Penguin Group (Australia), 250 Camberwell Road, Camberwell, Victoria 3124, Australia
(a division of Pearson Australia Group Pty. Ltd.)
Penguin Books India Pvt. Ltd., 11 Community Centre, Panchsheel Park, New Delhi—110 017, India
Penguin Group (NZ), 67 Apollo Drive, Rosedale, Auckland 0632, New Zealand
(a division of Pearson New Zealand Ltd.)
Penguin Books (South Africa) (Pty.) Ltd., 24 Sturdee Avenue, Rosebank, Johannesburg 2196,
South Africa

Penguin Books Ltd., Registered Offices: 80 Strand, London WC2R 0RL, England

While the author has made every effort to provide accurate telephone numbers and Internet addresses at the time of publication, neither the publisher nor the author assumes any responsibility for errors or for changes that occur after publication. Further, the publisher does not have any control over and does not assume any responsibility for author or third-party websites or their content.

First edition: December 2011

Library of Congress Cataloging-in-Publication Data

Holtje, James.
    The power of storytelling : captivate, convince, or convert any business audience using stories
from top CEOs / Jim Holtje.— 1st ed.
        p.   cm.
    Includes index.
    ISBN 978-0-7352-0460-7
    1. Business communication.   2. Communication in management.   3. Storytelling.   I. Title.
    HF5718.H634   2011
    658.4'52—dc23   2011030778

PRINTED IN THE UNITED STATES OF AMERICA

10   9   8   7   6   5   4   3   2   1

Most Prentice Hall Press books are available at special quantity discounts for bulk purchases for sales promotions, premiums, fund-raising, or educational use. Special books, or book excerpts, can also be created to fit specific needs. For details, write: Special Markets, Penguin Group (USA) Inc., 375 Hudson Street, New York, New York 10014.

This book is dedicated to my wife, Karin.
Thanks for the best second act anyone could ever hope for.

我愛你

Acknowledgments

I am indebted to several individuals who made this book possible. My father, Bert Holtje—an accomplished author in his own right—was the best sounding board I could have asked for when testing the idea for this book and at various stages throughout.

My literary agent, Ed Claflin—negotiator par excellence—made this book possible and was a truly helpful guide each step of the way.

My former boss, Jack Bergen, saw this book's potential right away and was more than generous in providing advice and writing the foreword.

Another former boss, Frank Ovaitt, was equally invaluable in providing suggestions and coaching.

I am also deeply indebted to my wife, Karin. She patiently endured my writing during the early hours of the morning before I headed to work, at night when I returned home, and on more than a few "lost" weekends.

All were encouragement personified.

Finally, my thirteen-year old son, Mark Holtje, who has already shown a strong interest in writing. I hope the family tradition continues.

Contents

Preface

The Power of Storytelling is designed to help you improve your business communications with ready-to-use stories and anecdotes. They can be used to complement your own stories, or in place of them. Either way, it's meant to help make your writing more compelling, more engaging, and more memorable by using one of the most time-tested arts available to any communicator—*storytelling*.

The book itself was borne of frustration. Not frustration with my profession—I *love* being a speechwriter and corporate communicator—but frustration with the lack of tools to help me do my job.

About two years ago, on a chilly Saturday afternoon in March, my wife and I were outside the Strand Bookstore on the corner of Broadway and 12th Street in New York City—a stone's throw from Union Square. For those not familiar, the Strand is a venerable New York institution boasting "18 Miles of Books," including a second-to-none selection of hard-to-find works. If bibliophiles were granted a taste of heaven on earth, this just might be it.

We've long had a weekend ritual of bargain hunting at the Strand's $1 remainder shelves outdoors. After peering down row after row of "gently used" hardcovers on this March Saturday, my eye was caught by one book in particular: the autobiography of an especially iconic CEO. I dipped in and read a few pages—and then some more. Page after page, what struck me were the *stories*. One more colorful and telling than the one before. The experience triggered a memory.

I thought back to a job I'd held not long before, as the English-language speechwriter for the CEO and president of Siemens AG, in Munich. One of my colleagues, an American who had settled in Europe and was writing speeches for the previous CEO at the time, once asked me if he could borrow some of the books I had brought from the United States when starting my three-year assignment. After much perusing, he thanked me politely, said the books were fine, but they were mostly quotations. He needed something different. He was looking for anecdotes, *stories*—particularly with a business slant. I had encountered exactly the same frustration in my own work. There are lots of quotation books out there, but not much when it comes to storytelling. And there's almost nothing when it comes to *business* storytelling.

That moment—standing at the corner of Broadway and 12th Street on that brisk Saturday morning—was my eureka moment. Wait a minute . . . Why not retell some of the best business stories right from the source—from autobiographies and biographies—and then collect them in a reference book for others to use? Instead of adding a quote or two in a speech, which might get a passing nod, why not add a *story* that will keep your audience's undivided attention?

I paid the princely sum of $1 for the autobiography, went home, and started putting ideas on paper. That's how this book was born.

It's my hope that it will be a constant companion and well-thumbed reference not just for speechwriters, but for anyone interested in communications as well as business in general. I hope it's added to your permanent collection. But I also hope it doesn't gather dust. It's meant to be used as a trusted source for ideas, a spark of creativity, a means for shifting your perspective, or, hopefully, a cure for the bane of all communicators: writer's block. Whatever the circumstance, it's designed to be *used*.

There's an old joke that you can always recognize a speechwriter in any audience. He or she is the only one *not* watching the person at the podium. Speechwriters are the only ones looking at papers in front of them, silently mouthing words a second or so before the person onstage actually utters them. True enough. And they're also usually the ones looking around the audience to see which lines worked and which ones—*well*—won't be included in future drafts.

I've observed more than a few audiences to notice something else. When people really pay attention, when the audience is really *fixated* on a speaker, when they're hanging on every word until the very end, more often than not, it's when they're hearing a story.

I've long believed that storytelling is among the most universal—and memorable—ways we have of expressing ourselves. Business has more than its share of great stories to tell. I hope this book can at least tell some of them.

Foreword

This book is for every leader, for one cannot truly be a leader without being an effective communicator. It shows how to draw on the most effective leadership communication technique in today's cacophony of messages and media—*storytelling*. It's also a book for those who help business leaders communicate: corporate speechwriters and business communicators. It's written and edited by one of the best speechwriters I have ever encountered, Jim Holtje, who has written for top business leaders in the United States and Europe. Like Jim, I am proud to have been a speechwriter and to share my reflections on this outstanding book.

Let me begin by telling a story.

In March 1983, President Ronald Reagan made an eloquent speech setting a bold vision of a defensive shield that would make "impotent and obsolete nuclear weapons." Skeptics and scientists, politicians and policy analysts soon attacked the idea with a wide range of arguments and dubbed it by the terrifying name "Star Wars."

As the administration began losing the war of words and the support of friends and allies, Secretary of Defense Caspar Weinberger decided to go on a speaking tour to explain and defend the concept. As his speechwriter, it became my job to help him prepare the speech.

We prepared a draft that thoroughly rebutted all the opposition's arguments. We quoted some of the president's stirring words from the original announcement and pulled in a quote from Winston Churchill supporting the need for bold action in time of crisis. Although Secretary Weinberger pronounced it a "solid speech," I had a sinking feeling that it was lacking the charisma and dramatic flair of Reagan. Secretary Weinberger would be unable to lift even the most stirring quotes into the headlines or TV sound bites. Instead, we faced a kind of trench warfare of words. Through the force of our arguments, we'd gain ground after each speech, but then the rebuttals of our many opponents would quickly be picked up by the news under the "Star Wars" headline and we'd be pushed back on the defensive.

In desperation, I asked Secretary Weinberger if he had any personal anecdotes he could include in the speech. He told me a story that he didn't think was very relevant. The story was about a conversation shortly after Reagan had lost his second Republican nomination bid in 1976. The two men were sitting in his study after dinner and Reagan, who had just turned sixty-five, was talking about retiring to his ranch. Then the conversation turned to Reagan's frustration that in losing the chance to be president he also would never fulfill his dream of marshaling America's industrial might to find a technology that would end the threat of nuclear war. It was that evening that Weinberger realized Reagan would do whatever it took to make that dream come true—including put aside his plans to retire to his ranch, so he could run for president again.

We encouraged Secretary Weinberger to talk about that fateful conversation in the speech he was about to give. Sure enough, when Weinberger opened his speech with that fascinating story, he created an emotional bond with the audience that set our arguments in a sympathetic context and allowed him to recapture the high ground in the Star Wars debates.

Besides the effect of that story on the audience, it also transformed an often imperious and intimidating defense secretary who was uncomfortable onstage into a relaxed and friendly human being. Since then, I've seen storytelling affect countless executives the same way. Perhaps it's their memory of reading stories to their own children that relaxes them and makes them more human. Or, storytelling could be built into the DNA of leaders—a legacy from ancient times when chiefs passed on the stories that formed the cultural foundations of their tribal societies.

But if storytelling is so natural, why then isn't it used as a communications tool more universally by today's business leaders?

There are several answers. It takes time to tell a story and executives often feel they must cut to the chase. Some leaders feel they must fit a predetermined image and that storytelling may reveal too much of their real selves. In a world driven by financial metrics, many businesspeople fear that intuitive approaches like storytelling may appear too soft or otherwise unacceptable within corporate customs.

This book takes on those feelings and fears. It shows us some of the most respected business leaders of our time using stories to communicate, showing us through their stories their paths to success. Instead of finding their stories, Jim Holtje could have interviewed them and simply listed their lessons learned for success. That would have been faster and more fact-based than learning through their stories.

But not as effective.

Because stories engage both the intuitive and the logical—the left and the right—segments of our brain, we are more likely to absorb and remember lessons via storytelling than through facts alone.

In a uniquely effective way, the book engages both sides of the brain for some of the most important lessons in business. In recounting a story told by a business leader, it appeals to our emotional self as well as the intuitive parts of our brain. It involves us in a personal drama with a setting, plot, and characters. Like a novel or a play, a story captures our imagination. Once we're hooked, the logical brain is engaged to reflect on the lessons, the wisdom, that can be drawn from the story. And, finally, the book guides us in applying that wisdom, the practical aspect. We are shown how to use the story and its lessons in our own communications.

The book works on two levels to help leaders communicate. First, it provides a selection of interesting stories and practical ways those stories and lessons of respected leaders can be reused in a leader's own communications. Second, it teaches leaders how to tell their own personal stories, which will be even more powerful than recounting someone else's tale. By sharing a story, a leader is building a personal connection that will drive greater loyalty from employees as well as greater acceptance from external stakeholders. And, when telling your own story, you'll be more relaxed, drawing on the psychic energy that comes from recounting an experience that you've actually lived.

Those who follow faithfully deserve leaders who are willing and able to inform—and perhaps even more importantly—*inspire* them. This is a book of stories told by leaders who met that standard and fulfilled that sacred obligation to those entrusted to them.

Jack Bergen
Vice President, Human Resources, Alcoa

Jack Bergen's professional communications career has included working for some of the nation's—and the world's—most renowned and respected political and business leaders. He has written speeches for U.S. President Ronald Reagan; Defense Secretary Caspar Weinberger; General Electric CEO Jack Welch; Siemens and Alcoa

CEO Klaus Kleinfeld; as well as other legendary leaders in the fields of business and government.

Bergen is the 2007 recipient of the Public Relations Society of America's Atlas Award for Lifetime Achievement in International Public Relations and was named by PRWeek *in 1999 as one of the most influential public relations professionals of the twentieth century.*

The Basics of Storytelling

People are hungry for stories. It's part of our very being. Storytelling is a form of history, of immortality, too. It goes from one
generation to another.

—Studs Terkel, Pulitzer Prize–winning
American author who specialized in oral histories

Storytelling is perhaps one of the oldest forms of communication
known to humankind. Whether it's a Hollywood blockbuster, the
latest bestselling novel, or a good yarn at a sales pitch, we're *hardwired*
for stories. The late Don Hewitt, creator and producer of CBS TV's
60 Minutes—one of the most successful programs in broadcast history and winner of nearly eighty Emmy Awards—said the idea for his
often imitated, but never surpassed program was simple—almost
deceptively simple. It was, he said, based on four words:

Tell . . . me . . . a . . . story.

And when it comes to stories, we listen. We tell our own. We almost
feel *compelled* to. Everyone's a storyteller whether one admits it or not.
In our own lives, events that happened yesterday, years ago, or decades
in the past end up being turned into *stories*. It's how we make sense of

the world and how we communicate that sense to others. While some are better at it than others, we *all* do it.

But business—the province of concrete numbers, logical analysis, and immutable facts—is often skittish about telling stories. That's a shame because storytelling is one of the most powerful communications tools we have. And some of the best business leaders have been outstanding communicators. Or, to put it differently, some of the best business leaders probably got to the top *because* they were talented communicators.

Either way, communication today is almost a job requirement for *every* businessperson. Whether you're heading a start-up in the basement of your home or heading a multinational corporation from a corner office high atop a skyscraper—or, most likely, you're somewhere in between—communication is part of your job. And a much bigger part than most people imagine. It doesn't matter if you're addressing thousands at an annual shareholders' meeting, giving a pep talk to your direct reports, or asking a single angel investor to buy into your dream. No matter the audience, no matter the venue, it boils down to one thing: getting your point across.

But not all communication is equal.

Consider the following scenario. Two companies—in the same city, same industry—are holding separate employee meetings at exactly the same time.

At Company A, the CEO enters an auditorium to an audience brimming with high expectations. Rumor has it the annual numbers are good—and they are. There's reason to celebrate. But as the CEO strides to the podium and looks out at his audience filled with beaming faces, he makes a fatal mistake.

He starts reading from a text-heavy, thirty-three-page PowerPoint presentation in a dry monotone, with all the enthusiasm of someone facing a root canal: ". . . and if you look here in the upper-right-hand quadrant, you'll see that the delta between last year's new orders and this year's was 7.8 percent, which was well within the range of our analogous industry peers. Now, in this slide, you'll see that we're on target vis-à-vis our three-year profitability projection, which I discussed in Q3 the last time we met . . ." And so on—and on—and on . . . People start to nod off. They're stifling yawns, looking at their shoes, scoping the exits. There's *no* connection. There's no sense the CEO understands his audience, or the commitment they've made all year that deserves to be acknowledged. The audience is not only bored—deep down, they feel *cheated*.

The CEO at Company B takes a different tack. It just so happens the past year was a success for Company B as well and the CEO there delivered similar numbers. But instead of thirty-three slides, she's got three. That's right, *three*. And instead of drowning people in numbers they can look up on their own, she quickly tells them the abbreviated results and then puts *their* victory in context:

"One of the reasons why the numbers are so good is customer retention. Let me give you just one example. Last month, I met with Chuck Smith, the CEO of one of our key customers in the Midwest, the PDQ Corporation. Some of you know we had some challenges with this account in the past, but I'm here to report we've made tremendous progress. When I sat down with Chuck, he told me how one of our generators had broken down last Christmas Eve. You'll remember that was the Christmas when it was about ten degrees below outside and the roads were icy and damn near impassable. Now, in the past, we all know what that would have meant . . ." Knowing smiles break out throughout the audience. She doesn't need to elaborate.

"But this time was different. Within an hour of putting out the call, one of our trucks was on the scene. The team got to work and quickly assessed the situation. Our quality initiative meant that they now had the most-used spare parts already on board. Long story short, they got that generator up and running in only an hour. Chuck paused for a moment after telling me this. He silently rummaged through his desk, uncapped his best fountain pen, turned to me, and said, 'Now, *where* was that contract renewal again?' Folks, that's why our numbers are up this year. The commitment each of us in this room made two years ago to improve service is paying off, one customer at a time. It's showing in this year's results, and this victory is *yours*. But we can't drop the ball now . . ."

Now fast-forward to later that day, later that week, or even later that year. Ask any employee at Company A what he or she remembers from that meeting. Is it the Q3 new orders figures? The annual R&D spend compared with 2010? The revenue generated from last year's new product launch? Or the fact that catering ran out of coffee? Most likely, the employee will remember next to *nothing*.

Now ask any employee at Company B what he or she remembers. While employees may not recall most of the numbers discussed that day, you can bet that most will remember the "Chuck story." And it will have become viral. It will have been repeated in break rooms, cafeterias, emails, on airplanes, at conferences, in conversations with spouses and friends, even to competing salespeople sitting down for a friendly beer. It will have taken on a life of its own.

Think about it. After all the herculean effort the corporate communications department put into gathering the data, confirming figures with finance, going through countless drafts of the speech, prettifying the PowerPoint presentation, does it really all boil down to a single story?

Quite often—yes.

Ask anyone who's been on either end of this scenario and that person will likely tell you the same thing: People really didn't start paying attention until the storytelling began.

Why?

As mentioned earlier, we're hardwired for stories. Just because you work in the hard-edged world of business doesn't mean stories or anecdotes suddenly have no effect on you. In fact, because most business audiences have likely spent the better part of their careers drowning in so many facts, figures, data, statistics, and oceans of other random information, most businesspeople are probably *starved* for stories to simplify the clutter. They're likely begging for someone to make sense of it all in a way that's clear, easily understood, and occasionally, inspirational. Facts without narrative are just that—random, unorganized facts. But facts set in a clear narrative can be the most powerful building blocks for effective storytelling—and thus, communication.

As mentioned earlier, the best anecdotes will always be the ones *you* can tell from your own experience, whether it was something you personally witnessed or an anecdote told to you by someone else. It's obviously easier to tell stories about incidents where you had some kind of involvement. You can add your own embellishments and—face it—it's easier to keep your own story straight!

This book is not about storytelling from your own life. There are more than a few great how-to books on perfecting your own storytelling technique. This book is about providing easily referenced anecdotes when you don't have personal material to work with.

Business audiences are hungry for authenticity and eager to hear a good yarn. Storytelling can be your secret communications weapon to give audiences what they want to hear. It can also help you achieve what you want most from your audience—not just applause, but that they *act on your words*.

PART ONE

Using This Book

The best anecdotes are *always* your own. Who better than yourself to tell a story that involves you? Who better to add touches of color and drama? Who better to keep the audience on the edge of their seats until that final line? But when you've got no material to work with— no personal reminiscences that fit—then this book can be a real help for your business communication needs.

It can be used in different ways. If you have the time, reading it cover to cover can offer a great overview of some really terrific business anecdotes, but certainly these aren't the only ones out there. You probably already have more than a few of your own, from books, articles, or personal stories you've heard through the grapevine. Not all of them will be included here, for the simple reason that it's impossible to cover them all. Plus, one person's "gem" is another's "yawner." No one size fits all.

You'll more likely be using this book as a handy reference when looking for an occasional anecdote to illustrate a point to be made in a speech, informal remarks, CEO blog, customer letter, PowerPoint presentation, company newspaper article, op-ed piece, letter to the editor, or some other form of business communication. I'm not sure an anecdote would fit in a Tweet—but you never know!

This book has several advantages over other reference works you might have used in the past. First, it is not a compilation of quotations. It contains anecdotes, which are longer than quotes and ultimately more compelling and more memorable for your audience. Second, it focuses on contemporary and near-contemporary business figures, so you're neither testing your audience's knowledge of history nor using examples that will seem out-of-date to present-day audiences. Third, it offers practical tips and suggestions on how to handle the material for your own needs.

The text is arranged alphabetically by business leaders' last names, with headings showing the various topics covered in each anecdote. Those same individuals and topics are also cross-referenced in the index. For example, you may want to look up an individual first if you need an anecdote from a particular person or someone from a specific industry. Or you may want to look first under the subject headings in the index and then find the appropriate stories. Use the index! It's designed to help you quickly find what you're looking for.

The chances are the story you're looking for will not come in its entirety directly from only one of the many anecdotes in this book. You have to be creative. Allow yourself the freedom to pick and choose as needed.

Writing—as you already know or will soon learn—is more art than science. *Your* needs will probably never be exactly the same as someone else using the same book or even the same anecdote. *It depends on the situation.* The key is bridging between your audience and the point you'd like to get across. Every circumstance is different. Sometimes it's the whole story, or part of it. Other times, just reading an anecdote sparks an idea and takes your writing down a more creative path you hadn't thought of traveling before.

Along with each anecdote in this book, there is also a separate section with suggestions on how to handle the story in your own writing. They're just that, though—suggestions. Feel free to use the anecdotes in ways that make the most sense for your individual writing needs. The story is already out there. How you use it is up to you. In all cases, however, it's best to use your own words so it's your voice making the connection, while remaining true to the facts of the story.

Most individuals cited in this book were chosen from lists compiled by business magazines and news outlets ranking the business heavyweight champions of our times. Others are equally well known in their respective industries. While not all are household names, they are names that should be familiar to most—if not all—business audiences. I've also generally chosen American CEOs—not just because they tend to write more books about themselves but also because they are more likely to be well-known to American—and even, for that matter, *global*—audiences. Connecting to your audience is critical. Citing business figures who essentially "need no introduction" is one way to achieve that connection right off the bat.

Most of the individuals cited are either still living or they made an impact on the business world sometime after the mid-twentieth century. From my own experience, citing individuals from earlier periods usually signals the beginning of a stale history lesson. Just hearing words like "As one Founding Father said after signing the Declaration of Independence . . ." is enough to trigger an incurable case of MEGO—"my eyes glaze over"—causing your audience to tune out fast. I happen to love history, but unless you're explicitly delivering a *history* lecture, sticking to contemporary—or near-contemporary—stories is a far better way to connect with modern business audiences. If you don't believe me, try adding a historical anecdote from the distant past to your next speech and watch the reaction. Be careful, though. They say yawning is contagious.

I've generally used more *autobiographies* by CEOs than *biographies*. Why? Autobiographies are straight from the horse's mouth—or at least as close to the horse's mouth as possible. While many business leaders covered in this book had help writing their autobiographies (CEOs are busy people, after all!), you at least know the material was approved. That's not always the case with biographies—especially unauthorized biographies. I felt it was best to use original material whenever possible, so the reader would know the source is legitimate.

I also hope the anecdotes in this book spark an interest in reading the original works from which they're cited. I encourage you to read them to learn more about the interesting personalities and their stories of overcoming adversity, as well as to gain insight and even inspiration.

Business books are a genre unto themselves, and the business autobiography may be its most compelling form. The stories business leaders have to tell us can be just as compelling as any by sports figures, politicians, celebrities, statesmen, military leaders, or other figures. Each of us is impacted on a daily basis by the decisions business leaders make—whether it's the products we buy, the services we depend on, the cars we drive, the food we eat, the high-tech gadgets we use, the media we consume, the companies we invest in or work for—in these and so many other ways, private-sector business profoundly impacts our daily lives.

And as you're about to find out, the individuals leading those businesses have great stories to tell.

Read on.

PART TWO

The Stories and How to Use Them

MARY KAY COSMETICS

Checking It Twice

> Efficiency
> List Making
> Productivity
> Work Habits

Mary Kay Ash, founder of one of the country's most successful cosmetic companies, tells of her habitual list making. She would write down everything that required follow-up, and the act of writing made it a commitment she had to address. She says the other advantage of list making is that it disciplined her to do the things she'd just as soon skip. The technique worked for her and she urged others to do the same.

She tells an old story she heard about Ivy Lee, a renowned efficiency expert from the 1920s. Lee met with Charles Schwab, then head of Bethlehem Steel, and had an offer for him. Lee said he could increase Bethlehem Steel's employee efficiency by 15 percent by spending just fifteen minutes with each of Schwab's executives. Intrigued, Schwab asked how much it would cost. Lee's reply? "Nothing, unless it works." Deal. Lee then met with Bethlehem's senior management and asked each of them to make him a promise. For the next three months, before leaving the office, they had to make a list of the six most important things they had to get done the next day at work in order of importance. Once done, the item was to be scratched off. If not completed, it made it to the next day's list. At the end of ninety days, Schwab was so impressed with the changes he saw that he wrote Lee a check for $35,000. The experiment worked. Writing was committing.

Using This Anecdote

Sometimes it takes an almost deceptively simple idea to contribute to solving a really complex problem. Clearly, Bethlehem Steel executives benefitted from the discipline of list making and sticking to written commitments. Do you? Try this: "I know how difficult it is to be distracted these days, but it pays to get back to basics sometimes. Management by objectives never really went out of style. In fact, neither did management by list making. There's a story Mary Kay Ash tells . . ."

Source
Mary Kay Ash, *The Mary Kay Way* (New York: John Wiley & Sons Inc., 2008), pp. 64–65.

Mary Kay Ash

MARY KAY COSMETICS

It's More Than Just Pink Cadillacs

> Applause
> Recognition
> Reward

Recognition is personal. It's been said that everyone's favorite words are his or her own name. And when people have worked hard, they crave recognition—especially when they know they've truly earned it. May Kay Ash says her company has made giving recognition to high achievers an important part of their management motivation. Aptly enough, the company even has a monthly magazine for independent beauty consultants called *Applause*, featuring sales successes and other topics. But when real applause doesn't take place for a job well done, Ash says people often feel something's missing.

She tells the story of being a guest speaker at a major manufacturer's conference. She had been invited to an awards dinner and noticed that several of the people sitting in the ballroom were wearing ill-fitting navy blue sports jackets. She turned to one of the executives and asked who these people were. He told her they were the company's top dealers. Throughout the dinner, Ash kept waiting for a speech and for the top sales folks to take the stage and say a few words. Instead, there was entertainment and the evening ended with a balloon drop from overhead. With the evening now wrapping up, Ash asked one of the executives whether there would be an awards ceremony. "Oh, they've already received their awards," he said. "The navy jackets we sent to their rooms." Minus some necessary tailoring and minus the chance to praise achievement in public where praise was due. In her opinion, this was a huge missed opportunity that she would have handled much differently.

Using This Anecdote

Real achievement deserves real recognition. But real recognition shouldn't be hidden from view. In fact, it should be out in the open for maximum effect. The awards dinner Ash details is about the polar opposite of how she handled recognition for her top performers. Try this: "Credit should always be given where credit is due. The recognition we're giving today is an important one for our company because achievement should never be left in the dark. Mary Kay Ash tells the funny story of an awards event she attended years ago . . ."

Source
Mary Kay Ash, *The Mary Kay Way* (New York: John Wiley & Sons Inc., 2008), pp. 34–35.

Mary Kay Ash

MARY KAY COSMETICS

Once You Get to the Top, Keep Moving

> Delegation
> "Executivitis"
> Failure to Grow
> Staying Sharp

You've arrived. You've made it to the C-suite or to the top of your division—or however you define the height of your profession. Is now a good time to rest on your laurels and enjoy the view? Maybe for a while, but definitely not for long. Self-improvement in any profession doesn't stop the minute you've arrived. Ideally, it should never stop, even after you've retired. Everyone needs to keep sharpening the saw. Managers continue to read about the latest trends in management journals, attend conferences, give industry speeches, go on customer calls, etc.

May Kay Ash tells the story of a former comptroller at a large corporation who came to her looking for a job. He had been very successful in his time. In fact, he had built his department to the point where he had delegated *everything*. That in itself is a great accomplishment, except for one thing: He failed to grow. He never bothered to learn about the new technologies that were revolutionizing his profession. The people working under him meanwhile became experts. Over time, he became far removed from the day-to-day operations of his own department. He ultimately—almost willfully—became obsolete and couldn't justify his salary any longer, so was let go. The irony is that the good habits that helped this person rise to the top were neglected once he got there, and they ultimately brought him down. Some diagnose this as "executivitis"—reaching the point where delegating ultimately puts you out of touch with the passion for the business that got you to the top in the first place. Whatever it's called, it's curable. It just requires staying sharp no matter what you do.

Using This Anecdote

It doesn't matter what profession you're in, you need to keep up with the latest trends. Just because you've doubled your staff or gotten a big promotion does not mean the world is going to stop for you. The same is true for companies in general, by the way. Try this: "Folks, these days standing still is falling behind. Companies can fall behind just like individuals if they don't stay current or lose touch with the daily operations. Mary Kay Ash tells the story of . . ."

Source
Mary Kay Ash, *The Mary Kay Way* (New York: John Wiley & Sons Inc., 2008), p. 149.

Mary Kay Ash

MARY KAY COSMETICS

Who's Putting Bread on Your Company's Table?

> Attitude
> Positive Reinforcement
> Sales
> Sales Organization

You catch more flies with honey than with vinegar. Mary Kay Ash tells the stories of two companies diametrically opposed when it came to their attitudes toward sales. She says she was part of a staff that had long been demoralized by management and its negative attitudes toward the sales force. She attended a meeting at which the company president gave a speech to his salespeople. For twenty minutes, he waxed lyrical about how wonderful the company was. He praised their products, their shipping, their warehousing, etc. This laundry list went on—until he got to the sales department. His tone suddenly changed. He began berating the group, saying that "if we had a trained dog to pass out brochures, it would outsell the best one of you." This negative attitude seeped all the way through the organization until it was in a virtual death spiral.

Ash contrasts that experience with another one she had at a banquet for a large manufacturing company. The CEO said that everyone was gathered tonight because of the sales department's great efforts. Yes, he also mentioned all the other positive attributes the company had, but kept coming back to sales. "But we all know very well nothing happens unless we sell somebody something," he said. Walking over to a blackboard, he then scribbled in big letters: "Production minus sales equals scrap." Ash says he clearly meant it. It doesn't take an MBA to figure out which company's sales force was motivated to work hard and achieve and which one was polishing their résumés.

Using This Anecdote

Positive reinforcement—without being naive about shortcomings—is a far better way to keep your sales force motivated than constantly pointing out shortcomings. After all, you could have the best product in the world, but if no one's buying, everything else is academic. Try this: "We need to go out there and sell like hell. But I want you to be very clear with your sales force: Headquarters backs you 100 percent and will give you whatever tools you need. I'm reminded of a story Mary Kay Ash once told . . ."

Source
Mary Kay Ash, *The Mary Kay Way* (New York: John Wiley & Sons Inc., 2008), p. 162.

Jeff Bezos

AMAZON.COM

Early Signs of Genius

> Tinkering
> Early Signs of Talent
> Engineering

If there's a gene for tinkering, Jeff Bezos must have it. The Amazon founder apparently has a history of inquisitiveness and a natural talent for experimenting that stretches way back. He recounts the story of being no more than a toddler and telling his mother that he wanted to sleep on a regular bed—no more crib for him! His mother told him firmly—"No." Young Bezos, however, didn't take no for an answer and decided to act on his own. He got hold of a screwdriver and patiently began taking the crib apart until it lay in pieces on the floor. Mission accomplished.

In another incident, when Bezos was older, he built a door alarm to warn him when any of his siblings were trying to sneak into his room. The family garage had already been turned into a laboratory and a place for numerous experiments, including a solar cooker and a hovercraft-like machine using a vacuum cleaner. During summers at his grandparents' ranch, Bezos learned how to lay pipe, repair tractors, and even use an arc welder—early signs of a tinkerer bound to experiment—and succeed—in creating one of the most successful online companies to date.

Using This Anecdote

Some people are late bloomers. Others show signs of talent earlier than the rest of us. Bezos's story can be used, for example, to encourage young people to pursue careers in the so-called STEM subjects (science, technology, engineering, and math). Try this: "This nation needs more engineers, more people who build and create businesses. If you're naturally inclined toward science, that talent can help you in a variety of career paths. I'm reminded of a story from Jeff Bezos when he was much younger . . ."

Source
Virginia Brackett, *Latinos in the Limelight: Jeff Bezos* (New York: Chelsea House Publishers, 2001), pp. 21–23.

Jeff Bezos

AMAZON.COM

Climbing a Steep Learning Curve

> Freedom to Fail
> Information Gathering
> Risk

Call it Gutenberg 4.0. It's easy to forget that in the early 1990s, the Internet was still virgin territory with lots of would-be millionaires but far fewer real successes. Jeff Bezos wanted in on the Internet revolution, but he followed a premise others often ignored. His notion was simple: Unless the new online platform created value for the customer, it would be better to continue the old way of doing business. He reasoned early on that bookstores could not possibly hold all titles in print nor could catalogs ever print anything close to a near-complete list. An *online* bookstore, on the other hand, could offer far more selection and add more value as a result.

He decided relatively early that his new Internet venture would sell books. One problem, though: He knew next to nothing about the publishing business. He needed to learn as quickly as possible. Doing a little research, he found that the American Booksellers Association's annual convention was being held soon in Los Angeles. He quickly booked a flight, and in no time, the inquisitive Bezos was roaming the aisles, visiting publishers' booths, gathering information from brochures, buttonholing eager salespeople, and even sharing his online plans with a few individuals. He climbed a steep learning curve fast and even found the answer to a key question of whether a database of books already existed, something he'd need to get started. The question now was executing his plan. By his own calculation, he reasoned that an Internet business had—at best—a 10 percent chance of succeeding. Not good odds. But because he had a great track record in reaching goals, he upped his chances of success to 30 percent. Still, he was betting on an only *30 percent* chance of success—worse than a coin toss! Yet, as he recounts, he actually found the chance of failure *liberating*—it freed him from the pressure of having to be a big hit. That freedom appears to have helped him immensely because a *big hit* is exactly what he got.

Using This Anecdote

It's hard to believe, but the founder of one of the most successful online bookstores (turned online seller of practically everything else) knew next to nothing about the publishing business when he first started. Bezos had the general idea of starting an Internet business, he just wasn't sure which industry to start in. Some firsthand research later and he was off and running. Try this: "Business is about taking risks. You may not realize this, but the founder of Amazon.com, Jeff Bezos, actually put the odds of his company succeeding at only 30 percent. He even started in an industry he knew next to nothing about. He tells the story . . ."

Source
Virginia Brackett, *Latinos in the Limelight: Jeff Bezos* (New York: Chelsea House Publishers, 2001), pp. 30–34.

Jeff Bezos

AMAZON.COM

"Go Back to Your Door and Work"

> "Location, Location, Location"
> Naming a Company
> Saving Money
> Start-ups

As start-up stories go, Jeff Bezos's account of founding Amazon.com has to be in a class of its own. He and his wife had already planned to enter the book business for their new Internet venture. The question was now *where* to locate the new enterprise. They were living in New York City but didn't think it was the right place for a start-up. Thinking strategically, they decided on far-off Seattle, Washington. Why? First, it had lots of IT, techie types. Second, there was already a huge book warehouse nearby in Oregon. The location had all the trappings of a ready-made "business cluster" as far as Bezos's plans were concerned. The only thing standing between him and his start-up's future home was twenty-four hundred miles.

Bezos loaded up his dad's Chevy Blazer and drove cross-country, where he and his wife rented a two-bedroom home in a Seattle suburb, paying for it with some of the seed money he had gotten from family. His new office? Just like the old days—a converted garage. To save money, he went to Home Depot, bought doors and brackets which he later fashioned into desks—not exactly mahogany furniture or a corner office . . . ! Next came the question of what to name their new venture. One of the first names he thought of was Cadabra, a variation on the word "abracadabra," implying a magical command. His lawyer thought differently. He cautioned Bezos that Cadabra sounded too much like "cadaver"—not exactly an appealing image for any company. They incorporated under that name anyhow but, three months later, decided to name the company after the world's second-largest river, with its seemingly endless branches and the advantage that its name began with the letter "A," which would place them at—or near—the top of any alphabetical listings of companies. Amazon.com was born.

Using This Anecdote

Jeff Bezos beat tremendous odds. Not everyone has the guts to go into a business he barely knew (books), move to a city far away from where he lived (Seattle), and come up with creative money-saving ideas (doors for desks) to keep expenses down. Try this: "I'm not asking for much when it comes to cost savings here, nor am I asking you to take tremendous risks, but I have to say I was inspired by a story I heard about Jeff Bezos when he started Amazon.com . . ."

Source
Virginia Brackett, *Latinos in the Limelight: Jeff Bezos* (New York: Chelsea House Publishers, 2001), pp. 34–36.

Jeff Bezos

AMAZON.COM

"I'm Working for This *Person?"*

> Customer Fulfillment
> Growing Pains
> Productivity
> Customer Service Culture

Start-ups are rarely glamorous. When Amazon.com was launched in July 1995, Jeff Bezos was amazed at the immediate customer response. Within the first month, they were getting orders from all fifty states—and some forty-five countries to boot. They were totally unprepared to deal with that kind of volume, however. Bezos soon found space for their offices in a two-thousand-square-foot basement warehouse that was only six feet high. He jokes that one of his first ten employees was six-two, so he had to walk around stooped all the time. During the day, they handled computer programming and other tasks. Afternoons and nights they would spend packing and shipping orders.

Bezos says the team would be kneeling on the concrete floor packing books, until one day he announced that his knees were killing him. His solution? Knee pads for everyone! Bezos says the person next to him cast him a look of disbelief that seemed to say: "I'm working for *this* person . . . ?" Another employee broke the ice in saying what they really needed were packing tables. They got their tables the next day, and productivity doubled overnight. In what may be the modern equivalent of starting in the mail room, Bezos says the fact that they were unprepared for such volume was probably a blessing in disguise because working with their hands and making sure all orders were personally fulfilled helped Amazon's founders form a culture of customer service early on that has long since dominated the company.

Using This Anecdote

Not every successful entrepreneur can claim that they spent their days writing code at a desk and their evenings packing books on a concrete floor. For Jeff Bezos and a handful of Amazon's first employees, however, it was a part of their early path to success. It also gave them an early taste of the company's entire value chain that few experience. Try this: "I know we can't all be a part of every single aspect of the company's value chain, but it helps to be close to the process so we understand it from all perspectives—including the customer's. I'm reminded of a story Jeff Bezos tells about the early days of Amazon .com . . ."

Source
Academy of Achievement, "Inventing e-Commerce," May 4, 2001, San Antonio, Texas: www.achievement.org/autodoc/page/bez0int-1.

Jeff Bezos

AMAZON.COM

"You Want to Do What?"

> Risk Taking
> Fulfilling Your Passion
> Thinking Long Term
> No Regrets

Go west, young man! Before Jeff Bezos founded Amazon.com, he was already on a fast track at several corporate jobs in New York City. While he was doing well in that world, technology still remained his passion. The spark of inspiration for him—his *eureka moment*—was actually a statistic. He had read that Internet usage was increasing 2,300 percent annually. That figure captured his imagination. *Twenty-three hundred percent!* Nothing out there even came close. He asked himself what would be the best business in this new and growing online environment. After much research, the answer he settled on—ironically—was perhaps one of the oldest industries around: books. The Internet would increase choice and offer more titles than any bricks-and-mortar store ever could. After thinking it through and talking it over with his wife, Bezos announced to his boss that he was leaving to start his own venture selling books online. His boss thought he was crazy. But after a two-hour walk in Central Park to talk about his idea, even his boss was convinced Bezos was onto something!

Bezos explains his decision to leave his job—in the middle of the year, before bonuses were given, no less!—as following what he calls a "regret minimization framework." He admits it's geeky, but it does reflect basic common sense. He essentially projected himself far into the future to age eighty. He then "looked back" on his life with an eye toward eliminating the number of regrets he'd hypothetically have. In his case, he says, he would have regretted not being part of the digital revolution and striking out on his own. Sure, he might have failed. But he would have regretted not trying even more. "If you think long term, then you can make really good life decisions that you won't later regret," he says. His advice to young people is simple: Do something you're passionate about, but don't assume that means chasing the 'hot passion' of the day. Bezos adds that we don't have a right to happiness. We have the "right to *pursue* happiness." What that happiness is only the individual can answer. And it's a lot easier to figure out if you calculate what you'd regret not doing looking back on your life from the future.

Using This Anecdote

Thinking with the end in mind is not a bad way to get perspective on just how much time you have left to achieve your goals—whether you're just starting out or contemplating a second or third act in business. Thinking long term and following your passion are good lessons not just for individuals, but for companies as well. Try this: "We should not pass up an opportunity like this one only to regret it down the line. I'm reminded of the story of when Jeff Bezos asked himself a very important question . . ."

Source

Academy of Achievement, "Inventing e-Commerce," May 4, 2001, San Antonio, Texas: www.achievement.org/autodoc/page/bez0int-1.

Jeff Bezos

AMAZON.COM

Put It in Writing

> Writing a Business Plan
> Getting Started
> Preparing Oneself Mentally

Watch the road. Jeff Bezos's famed cross-country trip from New York City to Seattle involved not only looking at the highway in front of him, but writing his business plan for even further down the road. In fact, he says facing a blank piece of paper and forcing himself to commit his ideas to paper constituted perhaps one of the *toughest* phases in founding his company. Along the way, he worked on writing what turned into a thirty-page business plan for his then still unnamed online bookselling venture. Once in Seattle, he says he handled what he calls housekeeping details, like incorporating the company, conducting the initial hiring, etc.

But Bezos knew very well that just having written a plan did not mean it would work in the real world. "You know the plan won't survive its first encounters with reality," he says. They rarely do. But it's unquestionably worth it. He says the discipline of writing forced him to think through issues more thoroughly, tossing out unworkable ideas and getting himself mentally prepared—imagining scenarios—for the cold dose of reality that he knew inevitably lay ahead. Daydreaming is fine, but turning daydreams into plans can only be done by putting your ideas down—in black and white.

Using This Anecdote

Writing works in other ways beyond business plans. It forces individuals to think through the logic of their arguments and commit their ideas to paper. What sounds like a great idea at a cocktail party or pitch meeting may not look as wonderful when actually committed to the printed page. Writing stuff down is actually a great way to avoid failure when no one's looking. Try this: "I'm all in favor of the great ideas we've been generating. But we need a solid business plan to back them up. Bull sessions without follow-up are just that—bull. Writing forces us to weed out bad ideas. Writing helped put Amazon on the map. I remember the story of Jeff Bezos's cross-country trip . . ."

Source
Academy of Achievement, "Inventing e-Commerce," May 4, 2001, San Antonio, Texas: www.achievement.org/autodoc/page/bez0int-1.

Cathie Black

HEARST CORPORATION

"The Purpose of This Meeting . . ."

> Leadership Qualities
> Listening
> Meetings

Hearst executive Cathie Black says that one of the critical skills a good leader needs to get ahead is the ability to listen. She tells an old joke from New York Yankees legend Yogi Berra, "You can observe a lot by watching," to make her point that leaders benefit greatly by talking less and listening more. And not just listening, but really *listening*— for tone, choice of words, clues where words aren't said, body language, places where a pause is needed or silence, etc. These are all part of communication.

She says that early in her career she heard a management consultant speak on the subject of meetings. The consultant said that three groups of people will be at any given meeting. The first group *has to*—they're required to be there. The second group *wants to* because being at the meeting is a vacation from whatever else they were doing. And the third group is essentially made up of *prisoners*—people who really don't want to be there. There are also different styles of participation. Some people are extroverts and speak often. Others barely say a word—but one should not assume they have nothing to say. Based on these observations, Black says she changed the way she conducted meetings. As a leader, instead of feeling she must be firmly in charge, she says her role now is to start the session by summarizing why the meeting participants are there and what they hope to accomplish. Then she actively listens to the conversation that unfolds—really *listens*. "Yes, sometimes leadership involves knowing when not to lead," she says. It not only encourages employees to become more actively engaged, but the leader learns more as a result.

Using This Anecdote

Everyone—not just executives—can benefit from listening more intently. It's been said that if you speak half as much and listen twice as hard, you will not only learn more, you'll be better perceived by others. Try this: "As future executives in this company, I can tell you from experience that communicating is a vital part of your job, but so, too, is *not* communicating. Holding back, for example, and letting your direct reports speak their minds can produce some amazing results while also sending the signal to even the most reluctant employee that it's OK to talk. Cathie Black tells the story of . . ."

Source
Cathie Black, *Basic Black: The Essential Guide for Getting Ahead at Work (and in Life)* (New York: Crown Business, 2007), pp. 240–241.

Cathie Black

HEARST CORPORATION

"More Shrimp?"

> Being Yourself
> Laughing at Oneself
> Mistakes
> Power

According to Cathie Black, one of the quickest ways to fail in business is to seek power for power's sake. It's also one of the quickest ways to drive a wedge between you and your management as well as you and your team. It is far better to focus on your strengths, work on your weaknesses, and let power follow as a result. She tells the story of being at an A-list party given by *USA Today*. She noticed that one of the executives had been busying himself during the event making sure everything was running smoothly. She went over to him and commented on how busy he seemed. In a theatrical but comic air, he replied: "I, too, have refilled the shrimp bowl." It got a big laugh from Black. As a powerful executive herself, she does much the same—pitching in whenever needed.

She also reminds people that you gain more respect if you can laugh at yourself instead of pumping up an ego that can only be publicly deflated. She tells of one such embarrassing moment when she was at a meeting of Coca-Cola's compensation board. It was the end of the meeting and her back was starting to feel sore, so she decided to take a pain reliever. She reached into her pill case and took two white tablets. By the time she'd swallowed the pills with water, it was too late. She hadn't swallowed painkillers. She had taken sleeping tablets instead! She quickly realized she'd most likely be asleep in about twenty minutes, and there was another meeting and a dinner yet to go . . . She slipped the chairman a note sheepishly explaining what had happened. He understood. A car was arranged, and Black was escorted to her hotel to sleep it off. Only someone comfortable with herself would ever share that anecdote in public—much less in an autobiography! No matter how high up the ladder you may be, to err is human. Pretending otherwise only tempts fate.

Using This Anecdote

Too many people buy into the image of power without realizing that's not how true power works. It can be a side effect of all your efforts to succeed, but it should not be the goal. The goal should be to succeed at what you're good at and be yourself through and through. Try this: "How many people here own up to their mistakes? How many of you are comfortable enough to laugh at yourself when you inevitably make mistakes? Cathie Black can. She tells the story . . ."

Source
Cathie Black, *Basic Black: The Essential Guide for Getting Ahead at Work (and in Life)* (New York: Crown Business, 2007), pp. 145–146.

Cathie Black

HEARST CORPORATION

"You've Come a Long Way . . ."

> Advertising
> Ethical Stand
> Feminism

Is your compass pointing true north? Cathie Black says the only compass worth following is an ethical one that upholds deeply held values. While working years ago at *Ms.* magazine, she says she handled the account with a major cigarette manufacturer who was beginning what was then a new campaign aimed specifically toward women—Virginia Slims. As one of the first magazines explicitly devoted to feminism, *Ms.* seemed a natural outlet in which to advertise. She met with the Virginia Slims brand manager, who said the cigarette maker was ready to make a commitment to advertise in the publication.

Black looked over their ads and thought they were fine. She then took them back to Gloria Steinem, the magazine's renowned founder. When Black showed Steinem the ads, Steinem told Black she was sorry, but they simply couldn't run them. Steinem had long been extremely vigilant about the magazine's brand identity, carefully monitoring stories, photos, and ads to make sure nothing contradicted that image. When Black asked why, Steinem answered that she felt it was condescending. First, the catchphrase "You've come a long way, baby" implied that smoking is a sign of progress—a message Steinem firmly rejected. Second, the word "baby," in her opinion, was infantilizing to women. In the end, a compromise was struck, with the magazine running a small calendar ad instead of the original ad copy. The tobacco manufacturer then decided to pull its advertising from the magazine altogether. In fact, they refused to advertise with them for the next *sixteen* years. Although she disagreed with her from a business perspective—lost revenue is lost revenue—from an ethical standpoint, Black learned a lesson from Steinem's decision. "*Ms.* survived the boycott with its mission, its conscience, and its readers intact," she says. In the end that also made business sense "since consumers tend to feel more loyal to companies they feel personally good about."

Using This Anecdote

Ethical decisions are rarely easy—especially when the bottom line is at stake. But they have to be made. As Black writes in recalling the lesson she learned, "While it's tempting to cut corners and push boundaries, it really is possible to succeed while keeping your ethics 100 percent intact." Try this: "We have obligations to live up to. I know this is not easy given the competitive pressures out there, but we need to think of the long term and what we ultimately stand for . . ."

Source

Cathie Black, *Basic Black: The Essential Guide for Getting Ahead at Work (and in Life)* (New York: Crown Business, 2007), pp. 248–251.

Michael Bloomberg

BLOOMBERG

Prepare for Landing

> Calm Under Duress
> Consistency
> Getting an Edge

Some habits are definitely worth keeping. When first elected mayor of New York, Michael Bloomberg was already a well-known public figure who had made his name building a business news empire and was an iconic entrepreneurial pioneer in his own right. Bloomberg tells of his persistent habit of seeking an edge that can one day help him. A licensed pilot, he recounts the story of taking his nephew for a ride in his private plane for a tour high above Manhattan. Not long after taking off from a local airport in nearby Westchester, Bloomberg's plane encountered engine trouble and had no thrust whatsoever. His aircraft had essentially become one big glider. Unable to fix the problem from the cockpit, he radioed the control tower saying he was returning immediately to the airport. The tower radioed back saying they would clear the runway and fire engines would be dispatched right away.

Never losing his calm, Bloomberg methodically went through his pre-landing checklist. His plane was airborne high enough to land without thrust—although he had only one shot at it. If he missed the first go-around, it would likely mean a crash. Intensely focused on the task ahead, he approached the airport, carefully brought the plane in for a landing, and came to an abrupt stop as rescue crews approached the aircraft. Everything ended well. Bloomberg says it was his consistent habit—time after time—of quickly gaining altitude right after taking off that likely saved him. Why did he do that? It always gave him more maneuvering room to land should the engine eventually fail. He says he made a habit out of doing this to get even that marginal edge just in case something like this were to happen—and sure enough, it did. Even if the margin is slight—whether in business or other endeavors—it can sometimes spell the difference between success or failure. Or, in this case, between life and death. "And if you never need it, that's even better," he writes.

Using This Anecdote

The practice and discipline of keeping an edge can always serve you well. Even if it's just a *marginal* advantage, you never know when it can help. Try this: "Our company has several advantages over the competition, but we need to keep the discipline of maintaining that advantage so we're not overtaken. Even small advantages count. Michael Bloomberg tells a story of exactly that and how this attitude likely saved his life . . ."

Source
Michael Bloomberg, *Bloomberg by Bloomberg* (New York: John Wiley & Sons Inc., 1997), pp. 217–219.

Michael Bloomberg

BLOOMBERG

When in Rome—or Maybe Not

> Diversity
> Global Business
> Sticking to Your Principles

Some principles need to be universal. Michael Bloomberg tells a story of the time when his media company was planning to launch operations in Tokyo. It was the company's first time breaking into the hypercompetitive Japanese market. He writes that he had had been given two bits of advice before breaking into a market long known as impenetrable to outsiders. First, find a local partner. Second, don't send any women. He thanked others for their counsel, and then . . . *well* . . . proceeded to follow his instincts and hired female staff anyhow! But would they fail because of that? Would it be committing such an unpardonable cultural faux pas that they would never be accepted? At the time, in the 1980s—and even more so before—most women in office settings throughout Asia were relegated to tasks like serving tea. Strongly committed to gender equality at home, however, Bloomberg saw no reason to suddenly adopt a totally different standard in a different country. He rolled the dice, and despite the advice, his Tokyo operations did just fine.

Bloomberg says he wanted each of his offices to maintain gender balance—regardless of location. After all, half the world's population is female and he'd like his two daughters to have the same chances as any male would have. He also sees it as a practical business issue. Advancement in the company should be based on competence—not chromosomes. If others wish to discriminate, that's their business. But if they do, ultimately it's their loss. "I hope our competitors always use some employment criteria other than competency," Bloomberg wryly adds. "We need all the help we can get!"

Using This Anecdote

Maintaining deeply held principles—like gender equality—even when it may not be popular or goes against conventional "wisdom" takes guts. The argument for gender equality in the workplace can also be seen as a business argument—after all, why cut yourself off from half of the world's talent pool just from force of habit? Try this: "We're committed to diversity at this company. For those who see this as a risk, let me remind you it's a business imperative that we advance all people based on merit. Michael Bloomberg, in expanding his business operations overseas, faced an equally tough challenge . . ."

Source
Michael Bloomberg, *Bloomberg by Bloomberg* (New York: John Wiley & Sons Inc., 1997), p. 172.

Michael Bloomberg

BLOOMBERG

It's Good to Work Hard but Better to Work Smart

> Hustle
> Keys to Success
> Outworking Others

Call it foreshadowing of a brilliant business career. Michael Bloomberg says one of the keys to success in business is to make oneself as *indispensable* as possible early in the game—then outhustle everyone else. He tells the story of a summer job he had between his first and second years at Harvard Business School. Bloomberg was working part-time at a small real estate office in Cambridge, Massachusetts, near Harvard Square. During the summer, students starting the semester later in September would often stay at nearby hotels while looking for accommodations for the coming academic year.

A keen observer, Bloomberg noticed a pattern. Would-be renters would often get up early in the morning to get a head start on the real estate listings. They'd call various agencies, set up appointments for later in the day, and then go back to bed. While his full-time, professional real estate colleagues started their workdays at the crack of 9:30 a.m., Bloomberg would be in at 6:30 a.m. He'd be just in time to answer calls from

all those early risers at nearby hotels. It worked. He says that throughout the day, his older colleagues would sit in wonder as person after
person would come into the office looking for him. Bloomberg says he
agrees with comedian Woody Allen's belief that 80 percent of success
is just showing up. Add outhustling everyone else and you've got a real
advantage. "You can't choose the advantages you start out with and
you certainly can't control your genetic intelligence level," Bloomberg
writes. "But you can control how hard you work . . . [And] the more
you work, the better you do. It's that simple."

Using This Anecdote

It's not enough to be bright; you have to put that intelligence to work.
Bloomberg's advice is simple: Watch what really happens in your market, find an advantage, and then act on it. Hustle trumps every time
winning ideas that never get acted on. Try this: "It's not enough that
we have better ideas, we need to outhustle everyone else. Michael
Bloomberg tells the story of a summer job he had between his first
and second years while earning his Harvard MBA . . ."

Source

Michael Bloomberg, *Bloomberg by Bloomberg* (New York: John Wiley &
Sons Inc., 1997), pp. 28–30.

Sergey Brin

GOOGLE

Truly Grateful

> Gratefulness
> Human Value of Technology
> Saving a Life
> Search Engine

Google's cofounders, Sergey Brin and Larry Page, say the motto for their company is "Don't Be Evil." Not exactly your typical corporate tagline. Perhaps easier to understand than "Be Good," but the phrase has still evoked an ongoing debate in the company. For both, however, it's clear that their search engine—the world's gold standard of search engines to date—is geared toward helping people make better decisions with better information. It doesn't mean all information is correct. But the same can be said of information in the world before the Internet, for that matter.

Brin and Page both say they often get letters from grateful Google users. One stands out in particular, however. Brin tells the story of a letter he and Page received from someone who said he was having chest pains and wasn't sure of the cause. The person did a quick Google search, compared his symptoms to the medical information he found online, and decided it was critical enough to go to a hospital right away. Sure enough, he was having a heart attack! He was quickly treated and survived. This grateful individual then wrote to Google's founders thanking them for giving him quick access to information he needed to make the right decision just in time. Without that access, the story might have ended very differently.

Using This Anecdote

Too many tech companies forgot about the human element. In their great rush to talk about features and how they were different than their competitors, they often forget about the impact they could have on people's lives. Google's cofounders have mentioned the story above in interviews as just one example of how technology can empower people for the better. Try this: "We need to communicate real value to our customers and stop talking about features only. For example, Google cofounder Sergey Brin tells the story of how their website . . ."

Source

Stephen Randall, ed., *The Playboy Interviews: Movers and Shakers* (Milwaukie, OR: M Press, 2007), pp. 128–129.

Sergey Brin

GOOGLE

The Melting Pot

> Immigrants
> Gratefulness
> Overcoming Adversity

Called by some a quieter, nerdier version of Steve Jobs, Google cofounder Sergey Brin says he was teased starting in elementary school, but he never let it bother him. His family had immigrated to the United States from Moscow when he was six years old. Brin's father was a math professor and the family says it suffered discrimination in Russia because of their religious heritage. Not exactly the best environment in which to bring up a family or in which to launch a promising career. As his father once told a reporter, "I was worried that my children would face the same discrimination if we stayed [in Moscow]. Sometimes the love for one's country isn't mutual."

Sergey says he had a strong accent when he first went to school—a source of the teasing among some of his schoolmates. Although he had friends, he was never exactly what you would call popular, by any measure. He never let it bother him, though, because he felt he was given a gift by emigrating to the United States and growing up here—

making him perhaps work and strive all the harder. "I know the hard times that my parents went through there and I am very thankful that I was brought to the States. I think it just makes me appreciate my life much more."

Using This Anecdote

Immigrants built this country and the new wave of immigrants like Sergey Brin at Google and Jerry Yang at Yahoo! are continuing to give this country an edge. Brin never let his feeling "different" get in the way of achieving his goals. It's not always easy to overcome these impediments, but it does speak to a spirit that should be honored. Try this: "Adversity is something we all face, but some have tougher odds to overcome. It's something we particularly see in this country's immigrants who bring with them the drive to succeed despite often facing more adversity than many who were born and raised here. Take Sergey Brin at Google, for example . . ."

Sources

Academy of Achievement, "Making the World's Information Accessible," October 28, 2000, London: www.achievement.org/autodoc/page/pag0int-1.

Stephen Randall, ed., *The Playboy Interviews: Movers and Shakers* (Milwaukie, OR: M Press, 2007), p. 116.

Warren Buffett

BERKSHIRE HATHAWAY

"Just the Facts, Sir"

It wasn't your typical intergenerational exchange. An amusing dialogue between Warren Buffett and a very young investor illustrates the point about making sure you've got all your numbers straight. At Berkshire Hathaway's 1990 annual shareholder meeting, Buffett opened the session to Q&A as he always does. Up stood nine-year-old Nicholas Kenner. Nicholas owned eleven shares of Berkshire Hathaway and asked Buffett, who was nearly six decades the boy's senior at the time, why the stock was trading so low, at $6,600 per share.

Buffett went on to answer the boy's question, but more importantly, he mentioned the unusual—yet charming—exchange in his next letter to shareholders. At the following shareholder meeting, Nicholas was back again, except this time he had an even tougher question. The young boy said that the annual report noted he was eleven years old when, in reality, he was only nine years old at the time. If Buffett got his age wrong like that, Nicholas wondered during the Q&A, how could he know the financials at the back of the annual report were reliable as well? Smart kid. Buffett, taking it all in stride, promised to answer him with a written response.

Using This Anecdote

It always pays to double-check your numbers. This humorous exchange between a precocious nine-year-old and the Sage of Omaha is a clever way to remind people of the simple truism that if one fact or figure you've used proves incorrect, the rest of what you've said or written could be called into question as well. Try this: "We need to make sure we have all our facts straight when we go out there and tell our story. Warren Buffett tells an amusing story of what happened to him one year at an annual shareholders' meeting . . ."

Source

Janet Lowe, *Warren Buffett Speaks* (New York: John Wiley & Sons Inc., 1997), p. 27.

Warren Buffett

BERKSHIRE HATHAWAY

Four-Foot-Ten and Tough as Nails

> Non-Compete Clause
> Taking Sides
> Respect

Rose Blumkin never graced the cover of *BusinessWeek*. But she was a major business figure by Warren Buffett's estimation. Those in the know knew that "Mrs. B" was an immigrant from Russia who had founded the Nebraska Furniture Mart in 1937, building it into the nation's largest home furnishings store. Her credo was simple: "Sell cheap, tell the truth, don't cheat nobody." Impressed by Blumkin's business acumen and the store's enormous success, Buffett decided to buy the store as a fifty-third birthday present to himself. He apparently walked into the store and asked her if Blumkin wanted to sell. She said yes. He asked how much. The answer: $60 million. No problem. Buffett left the store and came back with a check for $60 million. The agreement was only a page long. She said he was crazy not bringing lawyers, accountants, etc. But she cashed the check anyhow.

The two individuals' respect for each other only grew thereafter. In 1989, at age ninety-six, Blumkin left the business following a dispute with her grandsons. Bored with retirement and angry that Buffett didn't take her side in this ongoing family dispute, she took revenge on everyone and opened a competing furniture store across the street. She was ready to give Buffett and her grandsons a run for their money! Blumkin later resolved the dispute with her grandsons and forgave Buffett. Buffett, however, learned a valuable lesson. There had been a flaw in the agreement he signed with her a decade earlier. He should have included a lifetime non-compete clause so this situation could never have happened. His excuse? "I was young and inexperienced" back then, Buffett jokes.

Using This Anecdote

If you ever need to lecture someone on the need for being careful about contract language (especially non-compete clauses!), this may be the quintessential anecdote to tell. If the Sage of Omaha can learn a lesson about this important detail, then we all can. Try this: "When we sign this deal, we must think of every contingency, because the devil is always in the details. We certainly don't want to have happen to us what happened to Warren Buffett once . . ."

Source

Janet Lowe, *Warren Buffett Speaks* (New York: John Wiley & Sons Inc., 1997), pp. 38–39.

Warren Buffett

BERKSHIRE HATHAWAY

Saving for a Rainy Day

> Loss Liability
> Hedging Against the Unknown
> Insurance

Better safe than sorry. Warren Buffett says it always pays to be prepared for the "you-never-know" factor—even if it never comes to pass. Buffett says that he always sets aside a large reserve at Berkshire Hathaway for potential losses before year's end, for just that purpose. He cites examples of embezzlement at companies that don't get discovered until years later or losses on insurance policies from many years ago.

A story Buffett has told many times in previous letters to shareholders, to illustrate how the company estimates loss liability, is the joke of a person who goes on an important business trip to Europe. While there, his sister calls him with some bad news. Their father has just died. The grieving brother tells his sister that he's not able to get back to the States right away, but she should spare no expense when it comes to the funeral. He will cover everything once he's back. When he returns home, his sister tells him that the funeral was beautiful and presents him with a bill for $8,000. He pays up, no problem. The next month, he gets a bill for $10. A month after that, he gets another bill for $10. And the month after that—and so on. At this point, the man is totally confused. He thought he had already paid for everything. He decides to give his sister a call and asks her what's going on. "Oh, I forgot to tell you," she says to him. "We buried Dad in a rented suit."

Using This Anecdote

More joke than real-world anecdote, this is still a good story to remind people of the need to hedge against unknown negative factors that can swamp you in business. You may never need the money, but you never know. Try this: "We've had to set aside more cash this year because of all the unknowns in the marketplace these days. Some people have asked why. I'm reminded of a great story on this subject that Warren Buffett has told many times in his annual letters to shareholders . . ."

Source
Warren Buffett, Berkshire Hathaway Shareholder Letter, 2007: www .berkshirehathaway.com/letters/2007ltr.pdf.

Warren Buffett

BERKSHIRE HATHAWAY

It's Difficult to Teach a New Dog Old Tricks

> Age, Ageism
> Consistent Performance
> Experience

You're only as old as you as you feel. In his 1996 letter to shareholders, Warren Buffett talks about a deal he structured with a company called FlightSafety International, one of the world's largest pilot training companies. Impressed by the business, Buffett tells the story of meeting FlightSafety's then seventy-nine-year-old CEO, Al Ueltschi. The CEO had had a lifelong love affair with flying and had even piloted with Charles Lindbergh. He had a career as a barnstormer in the 1930s and later worked with the founder of Pan American Airways, Juan Trippe. In 1951, he built FlightSafety, creating flight simulators and training pilots. Quite an impressive record.

Buffett mentions that when they met, although Al was seventy-nine at the time, he looked and acted like someone no more than in his fifties. It wasn't the first time he had seen this type of vigor. He jokes that many of Berkshire Hathaway's hires, for example, look as if he and his partner, Charlie Munger, must have had a traumatic experience with an EEOC government directive from years ago not to discriminate against older workers. Not so, says Buffett. He says many of the Berkshire Hathaway managers who are over seventy are hitting home runs like they did decades before. Indeed, it is difficult to teach a *new* dog *old* tricks. He jokes that one way to get a job at the company is to employ the trick a seventy-six-year-old man used in getting a much younger, beautiful woman to marry him. His friends asked how he did it. Why did she accept? "I told her I was eighty-six," he answered.

Using This Anecdote

Although a little off-color, the joke's point is clear: Experience counts. With people living and working longer than ever before, it's important to remember that several generations will need to work together under one roof. What younger employees may have in verve and energy, older employees may have in experience and wisdom. A good time to tell this story might be when informing employees about hiring practices or the need to ensure the company has as many diverse skill sets as possible—not just the talents of one generation alone. Try this: "I recently read somewhere that in today's workplace, there will be five generations working together under the same roof. At Berkshire Hathaway, one of the most successful investment firms around, in fact, many of the employees are over seventy . . ."

Source
Warren Buffett, Berkshire Hathaway Shareholder Letter, 1996: www .berkshirehathaway.com/letters/1996.html.

Warren Buffett

BERKSHIRE HATHAWAY

Saving Money

> Cheap
> Deferring Gratification
> Saving Money

Call it hometown boosterism. In his annual letters to shareholders, Warren Buffett is fond of touting local Omaha companies where he owns a stake. One such store is Borsheim's. Founded in 1870, it's now one of the largest independent jewelry stores in the nation. The store has been a subsidiary of Berkshire Hathaway since 1989, and during the annual Berkshire Hathaway shareholders' meeting, Buffett is fond of mentioning that discounts are available for shareholders. In one letter, he says the company operates on a gross margin that's twenty percentage points below their competitors, "so the more you buy, the more you save—at least that's what my wife and daughter tell me."

Later in the letter, he tells a similar tale about saving money, saying that his wife and daughter were apparently impressed by a story from a long time ago about a boy who missed a streetcar on his way home. Rather than wait for the next one, he decided to walk home instead. When he arrived, the boy triumphantly told his father that he had just saved a nickel by walking home instead of taking the streetcar. Instead of praising his son, the father scolded him saying: "Why didn't you miss a cab and save 85 cents?"

Using This Anecdote

The references may be a little dated (American cities don't have street-cars anymore and 85 cents can't buy much these days), but the point is clear: If there's a better way to save money, do it. Try this: "I know we're under a lot of pressure to save money, but it's something we have to do. I know sometimes you get no credit for doing it, either. I'm reminded of an amusing story Warren Buffett tells . . ."

Source

Warren Buffett, Berkshire Hathaway Shareholder Letter, 2003: www .berkshirehathaway.com/letters/2003ltr.pdf.

Warren Buffett

BERKSHIRE HATHAWAY

Buyer Beware

> Mergers and Acquisitions
> Ruining Shareholder Value
> Fair Prices

Kiss any frogs lately? Throughout his many years as one of the world's premier investors, Warren Buffett has seen more than his share of acquisitions crash and burn despite the best efforts to put a positive spin on what clearly were bad ideas. He says in one year's annual shareholder letter that all too many managers have been caught up in the childhood story of the princess kissing the frog. In all too many cases, Buffett notes, the frog doesn't change at all—it *remains* a frog, just as some business ideas promise much in the future but don't deliver in the end.

Buffett says he's kissed more than his share of toads but has lived long enough to learn his lesson. He recounts advice he once got from a golf pro. The golfer, whom Buffett says wishes to stay anonymous, told him: "Practice doesn't make perfect. Practice makes permanent." Wise counsel for businesspeople and others alike. Taking the golf pro's advice to heart, Buffett says he then amended his own strategy when it comes to acquisitions: *Buy good businesses at fair prices instead of fair businesses at good prices.* Given Berkshire's track record, one can assume Buffett has indeed been following his own advice.

Using This Anecdote

It's a fact in the business world most people would prefer to forget: Most acquisitions fail. Even Warren Buffett admits to more than his share of clunkers. Even so, experience has been a wise teacher: A good price doth not always a good deal make. Try this: "I know this deal looks like a steal, but is it a bargain perhaps for a reason? Perhaps we should keep our eye on other factors beyond price and think of the bigger picture. Investor Warren Buffett once told the story of . . ."

Source
Warren Buffett, Berkshire Hathaway Shareholder Letter, 1992: www .berkshirehathaway.com/letters/1992.html.

Warren Buffett

BERKSHIRE HATHAWAY

Sleight of Hand

> Bait and Switch
> Intentional Deception
> Safekeeping

Not everything is as it seems—sometimes for good reasons. Warren Buffett tells the story of an informal group he was a part of that met every two years to have fun and discuss topics of interest among them. One year, they met at Bishop's Lodge Ranch in New Mexico. The topic they decided to discuss was the jewelry business. That year, Ike Friedman, the owner of Borsheim's, brought along some $20 million in merchandise from Omaha to dazzle the group and get the discussion started. The resort, a beautiful spot in the foothills of the Sangre de Cristo Mountains, was a great location for unwinding and talking in an informal setting. But as nice as the location was, Buffett knew that Bishop's Lodge was not exactly Fort Knox—especially relevant with $20 million worth of jewels on hand.

At the opening reception before everything got under way, Buffett discreetly told Friedman about his safety concerns. Friedman turned to Buffett and then pointed to a safe. "This afternoon," Friedman says, "we changed the combination and now even the hotel management doesn't know what it is." Buffett said he breathed a little easier after hearing that. Friedman then pointed to two armed guards standing in front of the safe. And the two of them would be standing guard all night, Friedman added. Buffett was finally at ease. He felt the party could now get started without a hitch. Then Friedman leaned even closer to Buffett and whispered into his ear, "Besides, Warren," he said, "the jewels aren't in the safe . . ."

Using This Anecdote

Like a page out of *The Art of War*, cloak-and-dagger deception is sometimes necessary when the stakes are high and you're trying to thwart those who would steal from you or take away your business. It could be a case of hiding your intentions to acquire a company or discreetly conducting due diligence; it could be the search for a new CEO while the current one hasn't yet announced his or her retirement—anything that can have material impact on the business yet needs to be kept out of the public eye. Try this: "I can't emphasize enough how important it is for us to be smart about our assets, such as intellectual property and so on. We're in a competitive business where the other guys are constantly looking for an edge to beat us in the marketplace. The last thing we need is to hand them what they're looking for. I'm reminded of an amusing story Warren Buffett told in this vein . . ."

Source
Warren Buffett, Berkshire Hathaway Shareholder Letter, 1989: www .berkshirehathaway.com/letters/1989.html.

Warren Buffett

BERKSHIRE HATHAWAY

"There's Oil in Them Thar Hills"

> Gullibility
> Herd Mentality
> Overvalued Stocks
> Rumors

Conventional wisdom can be just that—*conventional*. On more than a few occasions, Warren Buffett has leveled criticism against fellow investment professionals. He says you'd think that with their staffs of highly paid professionals they would be a force for marketplace logic, evenhandedness, and stability. Not necessarily. All too often, some of the most inappropriately valued stocks are actually those owned and monitored by large financial institutions. Rumors replace reason and "animal spirits" replace cold, hard logic.

Buffett tells a joke a friend related to him illustrating the type of behavior investment pros all too often engage in. An oil prospector dies and goes to Heaven. He's met at the Pearly Gates by St. Peter, who has good and bad news. The good news is he's been accepted into Heaven. The bad news is there's no space right now. The prospector looks around, and sure enough, the area reserved for oilmen is packed—not an inch to spare. He thinks about it for a moment, then turns to St. Peter and asks him if he could just say one thing to those already there. St. Peter doesn't see the harm, so he lets him approach the group. The prospector cups his hands and yells, "Oil discovered in Hell!" and the place clears out! Impressed, St. Peter beckons the prospector inside. The prospector then turns to St. Peter and says, on second thought, "I think I'll go along with the rest of the boys. There might be some truth to that rumor after all."

Using This Anecdote

In the absence of solid information, rumors take on a life of their own—no matter what the industry. Buffett's joke is a good one for illustrating how people—more often than they're perhaps willing to admit—move more with the herd than by trusting their own reason. Better to be wrong with the rest of the group than run the risk of being wrong and standing alone. Try this: "I know there's always the temptation to follow the crowd, and we hear a lot about the wisdom of the crowd, but sometimes the crowd is wrong. Warren Buffett tells a great joke about being careful of putting too much trust in conventional wisdom . . ."

Source
Warren Buffett, Berkshire Hathaway Shareholder Letter, 1985: www .berkshirehathaway.com/letters/1985.html.

Michael Dell

DELL INC.

Talk Among Yourselves

> Customer Research
> Getting Candid Advice
> Peer-to-Peer Communication

Call it third-party candor. Dell Inc. had long been a leader in listening to customers and cutting out the middleman. Michael Dell tells the story of a successful idea he implemented called "Platinum Councils"—regional meetings held worldwide with key business customers every six to nine months. These are not your typical one-on-one get-togethers, however. They're based instead on a fascinating observation: Customers tend to speak more candidly and honestly peer-to-peer among themselves than they necessarily would meeting one-on-one with suppliers, like Dell, with whom they have a business relationship. One such meeting—with several different customers in the room—produced an absolutely critical insight Dell believes possibly saved the company billions.

His desktop engineers had been redesigning models based on the premise that they thought business customers wanted *faster* performing systems, just like consumers. The discussions at the Platinum

Councils, however, pointed in a completely different direction. While no one denied that improving performance would be nice, what counted more for these top business customers was a stable, reliable product. This was especially true for industries, like finance and airlines, where reliability was mission-critical. The engineers were overruled. The response was to focus instead on reliability for corporate clients while focusing on speed for the consumer market. What seemed like a miscommunication between engineers and business customers was solved by listening to what customers really wanted. Yet this insight might never have seen the light of day were it not for the fact that it was given the right environment in which to occur. Only then could the company get the candid answers they were looking for—not the answers customers thought Dell wanted to hear.

Using This Anecdote

By getting customers together on a peer-to-peer basis, Michael Dell was able to find a key insight that he wouldn't necessarily have found in the usual one-on-one meetings. Try this: "Do we understand what our customers really need? Or are we going by what we *think* they need? Let me tell you a story about how Dell gained some amazing insights by stepping back from one-on-one conversations and instead letting customers talk among themselves . . ."

Source

Harvard Business Review: Interviews with CEOs (Cambridge, MA: Harvard Business School Press, 2000), pp. 128–130.

Michael Dell

DELL INC.

The Precocious Third Grader

> Eliminating Unnecessary Steps
> Efficiency
> Supply Chains

Unnecessary steps are just that—*unnecessary*. Michael Dell built a high-tech empire largely by eliminating the middlemen, who bogged down other computer manufacturers, and instead enabling customers to custom-order their computers. Dell writes that he had long been fascinated with the idea of eliminating unnecessary steps and driving as much efficiency as possible, even from a *very* early age. He tells a story of when he was in the third grade. He had seen an ad on the back of a magazine touting how to earn a high school diploma by taking a simple test—clearly some kind of equivalency exam. Young Dell was intrigued. While education had long been a priority in his family, and he had had a lifelong love of learning instilled in him early on, he was also impatient. He reasoned that if he passed the test, he could eliminate the need for nine more years of schooling and move ahead that much faster!

He sent in the form and waited. Not long afterward, a representative from the testing company came to the Dell house one evening. Michael's mother answered the door. The company rep asked if she could speak with a "Mr. Michael Dell." His mother was puzzled. She said her son was taking a bath right now, but she would go get him. A few minutes later, eight-year-old Michael Dell emerged wearing a bathrobe. Needless to say, this wasn't exactly what the company rep had expected. When everything was eventually sorted out, Michael's parents and the woman from the testing company had a big laugh over this precocious third grader's audacious plan. He wanted not just to skip to the head of the class—but to skip all of the classes in front of him! Dell obviously went on to complete his education, but after that incident, he wasn't surprised he ended up where he did. "Since an early age I've been fascinated with the idea of eliminating unnecessary steps. So I guess I'm not surprised that I started a company based on eliminating the middleman."

Using This Anecdote

Eliminating unneeded steps is critical for boosting efficiency and a key message for any business leader. When telling the story, you're obviously not advocating that people cut their academic careers short. But you are urging them to think along the lines that made Michael Dell enormously successful. If steps can be eliminated to drive efficiency without sacrificing quality, by all means, do it! Try this: "We need to drive greater efficiency in our supply chains and be as lean as possible. If steps are unnecessary, we need to eliminate them. Michael Dell tells a great story about just this subject from early on in his life . . ."

Source
Michael Dell, *Direct from Dell* (New York: HarperBusiness, 1999), pp. 3–4.

Michael Dell

DELL INC.

Go Global, Young Man!

> Believing in Your Business Model
> Going Global
> Not Listening to Naysayers

It *is* a small world after all. By the end of 1986, Dell was raking in about $60 million in sales annually. Great, but the goal they had set was $1 *billion* by 1992! One way to achieve that ambitious objective was to translate Dell's explosive growth in the United States into expansion overseas. The decision was made to enter international markets—but not blanket the entire globe. Canada seemed the most logical next step, but Europe promised bigger returns . . . Michael Dell decided to start with the UK. Two years before, he had been to London for a family trip during spring break of his freshman year of college. While in the British capital, he'd visited several computer stores, taking note of the exact same phenomenon he witnessed in America: poor service and high product markups. Just as in the United States, there were many Britons who wanted computers but were unhappy with what the marketplace was offering them. Bottom line: There was *demand* for what Dell had to offer.

When Dell opened his UK business in the summer of 1987, he held a press conference to announce the news. Virtually every journalist who showed up was convinced Dell would fail. Their reasoning? While the direct-buying model may have worked well in the United States, it could never be transplanted to the UK. Buying directly from the manufacturer was not something the British were used to doing. But the company's UK business was profitable virtually from the get-go. As Dell expanded into other parts of Europe, the nay-saying continued, only to die down once most of Europe was covered. But—lo and behold—it reared its ugly head again when Dell announced plans to expand into Asia. But even there, the same story played out and success followed. Ultimately, it's the *customer* who decides what works—not naysayers who often only look in the rearview mirror, instead of much farther down the road. For Michael Dell, the lesson learned was simple: "Believe in what you're doing. If you've got an idea that's really powerful, you've just got to ignore people who tell you it won't work, and hire people who embrace your vision."

Using This Anecdote

A good idea is usually a good idea in any part of the world, whatever the differences. As long as the basic business concept is sound, unless somebody presents convincing arguments to the contrary, criticism is usually little more than hot air—or unfounded jealousy. Just because one way of doing things has been in existence for years doesn't mean you can't do it in a better or more efficient way. After all, there's no progress without change. Try this: "I know we've had some bumps in the road as we've expanded overseas, but I'd like to remind everyone that whatever differences there may be, there's no debating a good business idea in any language. For example, consider what happened to Michael Dell early in his career when he was already expanding his business overseas . . ."

Source

Michael Dell, *Direct from Dell* (New York: HarperBusiness, 1999), pp. 27–29.

Michael Dell

DELL INC.

If You Want Your Change Back, Go Ask the CEO

> Delegating
> Growing Pains
> Letting Go

At some point, you have to let go. As Dell Inc. went from a small start-up to a multinational success, Michael Dell went through a lot of trial and error to get the right systems in place to operate more efficiently. One of the biggest lessons he learned early on was the art of delegation. When the company was small, he needed to do virtually everything himself. As it grew, though, he quickly realized he needed to delegate, otherwise the business would suffer.

When he started the business, Dell was still used to keeping the schedule of a college student: late to bed, late to rise—the polar opposite of Ben Franklin's sage advice! If he overslept, he'd groggily show up to work, meeting some thirty employees cooling their heels outside a locked door waiting for Dell to let them in. He finally surrendered the keys to someone else, thus ending his doorman duties. In another incident, Dell says he was engrossed in solving a complex problem, when an employee walked in saying he had just lost money in the

Coke machine. Dell, flustered by the interruption, asked him why he was telling him. The employee answered: because he wanted his money back and Michael had the key to the Coke machine! It was at that moment, says Dell, "that I learned the value of giving someone else the key to the Coke machine"—and the value of letting go and delegating to others.

Using This Anecdote

It's impossible for executives to do everything—and do it well—all by themselves. This is just as true for start-ups as it is for major organizations. An experienced manager knows that delegation is part of the job. Holding on to everything only delays the inevitable. Try this: "We are growing far too fast to possibly keep doing everything by ourselves. We need to let go and delegate to others or find other people to handle certain things. I'm reminded of a story Michael Dell tells about the early history of his company . . ."

Source
Michael Dell, *Direct from Dell* (New York: HarperBusiness, 1999), pp. 17–18.

Michael Dell

DELL INC.

A Whole Floor for This?

> Observing
> Understanding Customer Demand
> Visiting the Customer

When was the last time you saw your customers on their home turf? Michael Dell tells the story of visiting a customer in the energy business in the UK in the late 1980s when the London real estate market was white hot and space was at an absolute premium. The customer had dedicated an *entire floor* of its London headquarters just for the IT department to assemble and configure computers. Dell was amazed to see employees busily unpacking computers, loading software, adding network interface cards, removing features they didn't need, etc. Given London's astronomical real estate prices, he couldn't help but wonder if this was the best use of an entire floor of office space!

As he was observing people scurrying around him, the IT person showing him around asked Dell if Dell Inc. could do this for them since they had no intention of becoming a computer company. Dell answered that they'd be happy to. He then followed through on the promise, quickly leading not only to a deepening of the relationship with this customer, but also to the creation of a new systems integration line of business. For Dell, the key was going to the customer's home turf and actually seeing how they really conducted business. Not listening to them tell you how they work, in one of your plush conference rooms or corner offices—but seeing how it's done in *their* world. Needless to say, it was an eye-opener. "By spending time with your customers where *they* do business, you can learn more than bringing them to where *you* do business."

Using This Anecdote

It's not enough to have your customers visit you; you have to go to the customer to experience up close and personal what challenges they face. First, the customer appreciates the gesture. Second, by carefully observing, you can not only find new ways to better serve *that* customer, you may get the creative spark you need to find game-changing solutions to benefit all your customers. Try this: "How many people in this room have been on-site with their major customers recently? If not, I want you to be. We need to know what our customers face where they do their business. Michael Dell tells the story . . ."

Source

Michael Dell, *Direct from Dell* (New York: HarperBusiness, 1999), pp. 158–159.

Michael Dell

DELL INC.

Pride Comes Before a Fall

> Accepting the Status Quo
> Believing Your Own Press

There's nothing wrong with being proud of your company's accomplishments. But there is something wrong with letting that pride convince you the status quo will last forever—or that you will always have the advantage. That often leads to a false sense of security that lulls you into thinking you're invincible and can blind you to opportunities to improve and grow the business. Michael Dell's example? A person who, in 1986, graced the cover of *Fortune* magazine billed as "America's most successful entrepreneur."

The winner of that appellation at the time was the then CEO of Digital Equipment. This high honor didn't last long, however. Partly because Digital Equipment held on to a proprietary system of its own and never successfully made changes to make their equipment compatible with evolving industry standards, so Digital's stock collapsed. It fell from $200 to about one-tenth that amount, only to go up again briefly before the company was eventually taken over—lock, stock, and barrel—by Compaq. A major player in the American computer market for decades, by 1998, it had fallen off the radar screen alto-gether. "Being on the cover of *Fortune* doesn't guarantee you any-thing," says Dell. Resting on one's laurels is nice for a while, but rest too long and your competitors will pass you by.

Using This Anecdote

Pride almost always comes before a fall. Although you may have achieved something big—an industry award or a cover-page profile—it should never trigger complacency or be an excuse to let down your guard. Be careful of believing too much of your own press as well. It has a way of catching up with you. Try this: "This is a terrific accom-plishment and we should all be proud. But we have to remember, this only raises the bar and becomes the new baseline. We can't now sit back and coast from here on in. I'm reminded of a story Michael Dell told on this subject . . ."

Source
Michael Dell, *Direct from Dell* (New York: HarperBusiness, 1999), pp. 128–129.

Michael Dell

DELL INC.

Sticking to What You Know Best

> > Exit Strategy
> > Focusing on Core Business
> > Sticking to the Original Game Plan

Mistakes happen. The trick is moving on. By 1994, Michael Dell's retail business was growing at a brisk 20 percent annually. Still, the move into bricks-and-mortar retail, working with such partners as Circuit City and CompUSA, represented a major departure from the original—and successful—model of dealing directly with the customer. It was, after all, that model that set Dell apart in the first place. Dell tells the story of how he then scrutinized the retail numbers more closely. Despite strong sales, they weren't making any money. Margins were too thin. If that was the case with their company, he concluded, it must be true for competitors as well. A decision was made to put this line of business on notice: They had better justify their numbers or the plug would be pulled. The retail division responded by expanding into Walmart and Best Buy, but it was no use. With retail representing such a small portion of sales, the decision was made to exit that segment altogether.

The reaction was swift. Analysts said Dell was making a mistake—needlessly limiting future growth. But Michael Dell had the numbers on his side. Media firestorm aside, the move had a major, perhaps unintended effect on the company. By exiting what had been unfamiliar territory, the company was forced to focus 100 percent on its original model of selling directly to the customer—where it was most profitable and where it held an advantage. Instead of dividing time between retail *and* direct, employees could now focus on what they knew best and where they were most profitable. As Dell sees it, "They were grateful for the clarity that getting into—and out of—retail had afforded," he writes. Experiment over, Dell didn't look back.

Using This Anecdote

Sometimes subtraction is more important than addition in business. While sales numbers looked good, a root P/L analysis showed that this line of business was not making Dell any money. How long could that last? Sometimes it makes sense to ignore the pundits, exit a line of business outright, recoup your losses, and refocus on what you do best. Try this: "I know this is not an easy decision, and many of you are disappointed we're exiting this market, but we need to look at the bigger picture. I'm reminded of a story that Michael Dell tells . . ."

Source
Michael Dell, *Direct from Dell* (New York: HarperBusiness, 1999), pp. 76–78.

DELL INC.

One Last Item, If You Have a Moment . . .

> Market Differentiator
> Game-Changing Technology
> Risk

You never know where the next game-changing idea can come from. Michael Dell tells the story of how his company happened upon using long-lasting lithium ion batteries—almost by accident. Dell had been in Japan shortly after the company launched operations there. He was meeting with Sony to talk about monitors, CD-ROM drives, and other technologies Sony was developing. During the course of the meeting, someone from Sony's energy power systems division said he wanted to speak with him afterward. At first, Dell was confused. Energy systems? What would they possibly talk about? Dell wasn't in the power plant business after all. It sounded like this guy was about to waste his time.

Indulging this eager Sony employee, Dell listened patiently. Turns out, it was a good move. Dell soon learned that Sony had been developing a new lithium ion battery that had the potential to last longer and weigh significantly less. Sony was already looking to use it in smaller devices and saw laptops as a new market as well. Dell immediately saw this as a potentially game-changing breakthrough technology and moved forward quickly. It was a risky proposition, though. They had to choose between the new and untested technology and the existing nickel hydride. A year and a half after that spontaneous conversation in Japan, the first Dell laptops with lithium ion batteries were introduced—an industry first—in a media event in August 1994 in which a laptop was run on battery power on a nonstop flight from New York to Los Angeles. Five and a half hours later, the laptop had broken all records, and it went on to become the industry standard. A rushed conversation that almost didn't happen had led to a move that leapfrogged the competition. You never know.

Using This Anecdote

You need to hear people out because you never know where the next winning idea may come from. Listen carefully and try connecting dots where others can't—or won't. Remind people that sometimes you have to take big gambles in order to get a jump on your competitors. In Dell's case, no one had been using this technology, so it *was* a gamble. But it was a gamble worth taking. Try this: "You never know where our next great game-changing idea can come from. It pays to listen closely. Michael Dells says . . ."

Source
Michael Dell, *Direct from Dell* (New York: HarperBusiness, 1999), pp. 53–55.

Michael Eisner

THE WALT DISNEY COMPANY

Bonsoir, Mr. President

> Endorsements
> Marketing
> Political Favors
> Public Relations Coup

It helps to have friends in high places. Former Disney CEO Michael Eisner tells the story of Disney's push to reinvigorate their theme parks, especially Disneyland Paris, which had been struggling since opening in 1992. By dropping prices, boosting marketing, and cutting overhead, they were starting to make progress, but the needle wasn't moving fast enough. Eisner says that in spring 1994 he was with former U.S. president George H. W. Bush at a performance of *Beauty and the Beast* in Houston, Texas, when the conversation eventually turned to the challenges Disney was facing at their Paris theme park. Eisner told "Bush 41" that French president François Mitterrand—who was not exactly known as a connoisseur of American pop culture—kept refusing to visit the park.

The elder Bush said that he was longtime friends with Mitterrand. Already planning to visit Europe with his children and grandchildren, he said he would invite the French president to dinner at the theme park. Sure enough, the former president was good to his word. Mitterrand and Bush dined at L'Auberge de Cendrillon inside the park. When the two statesmen emerged from the restaurant to a waiting press corps, Eisner recounts how the former American president turned to Mitterrand and said: "Smile. Come on, François, *smile!*" Sure enough, the dour defender of elite French culture grinned for the cameras in front of the iconic Disney castle, a symbol of American popular culture. That shot made it to the front page of every newspaper in France the next day—at the height of the tourist season no less! From a president who set his country's cultural agenda, there could have been no bigger or better symbolic endorsement.

Using This Anecdote

An endorsement, even if it's only implied, can be worth its weight in gold. Of course, it doesn't have to be from a head of state; it can be from a key customer, or a significant figure in your industry. Try this: "The endorsement we got today from X is really significant. It shows a lot of creativity in how we go about winning endorsements from even our most challenging customers. In fact, because X was seen as so challenging, today's news is all the more valuable. It reminds me of a story Michael Eisner told . . . If Bush can get Mitterrand to smile, we sure as heck didn't need to work as hard to get today's endorsement . . ."

Source
Michael Eisner, *Work in Progress* (New York: Random House, 1998), pp. 398–399.

Michael Eisner

THE WALT DISNEY COMPANY

"I'm Going to Disneyland!"

> Advertising
> Catchphrase
> Spontaneity
> Spousal Input

It went on to become an iconic phrase. It's often repeated and always associated with the brand. An athlete just wraps up a winning game. A voice offstage asks what he or she is going to do next, and the athlete says, "I'm going to Disneyland!" The interesting story behind that iconic phrase is that it didn't come from a focus group or months of marketing research. It started as a simple conversation among people who weren't even Disney employees. Former Disney CEO Michael Eisner tells the story of when he and his wife were joining George Lucas and others at a dinner to promote the opening of Star Wars Tours.

Also at the dinner were Jeana Yeager and Dick Rutan, who had become famous for piloting a single-engine plane around the world on one tank of gas. During the evening, Eisner's wife, Jane, was making small talk with the pair when she turned to them and asked what were they going to do next, now that they had achieved such an amazing feat. "Well, we're going to Disneyland" came the answer in all sincerity. Jane liked the phrase so much she told her husband, adding that this would make a great ad campaign. The next morning, Eisner was on the phone with his marketing people, and two weeks later, Giants quarterback Phil Simms was smiling for the camera saying "I'm going to Disneyland!" just after winning the Super Bowl. Not many campaigns have such a short turnaround—or such resonance.

Using This Anecdote

Creative ideas can come from sources or moments that just can't be planned. Of course, being the wife of the CEO helps, but still . . . This idea not only came from someone who wasn't an employee, but also it was executed brilliantly within what must have been record-breaking time. Try this: "We need more creativity, more spontaneity, and quicker turnaround at this company. We all know the 'I'm going to Disneyland' phrase, but what you may not know is where that phrase came from and how quickly it was set into motion. Michael Eisner tells the story of when . . ."

Source

Michael Eisner, *Work in Progress* (New York: Random House, 1998), pp. 212–213.

> Branding
> Cultural Differences
> Marketing

What's in a name? Often—*a lot*. When Disney first built its theme park in France, it was called Euro Disney. Former Disney CEO Michael Eisner tells the story of how plenty of mistakes had been made along the way with the new park, but one in particular had to be quickly corrected. For Americans, the word "Euro" had long been associated with a continent seen as glamorous, cultured, and sophisticated. For this iconic U.S. company, it made perfect sense to tap into that image and name the park Euro Disney. Americans would love it.

But there was a problem. The park wasn't designed primarily to attract American tourists traveling overseas. It was designed mainly for the French and other Europeans looking for a taste of America. Worse, for most Europeans, the word "Euro" was *anything* but glamorous. It was the name of the continent-wide currency about to be launched. It stood for business and commerce, not to mention faceless bureaucrats in Brussels. Not exactly anyone's idea of Disney's brand association, generally thought of as fantasy, make-believe, and dreams coming true. It didn't take long before the Euro Disney signage came down and up went Disneyland Paris. Eisner says the name change not only helped them better identify with founder Walt Disney's brand identity for the original park but also added the associated cachet of one of the most romantic cities in the world.

Using This Anecdote

What seems like a good idea can sometimes collide with the realities of the marketplace. All too often, planning reflects our own narrow perspective on the world, instead of reflecting what the world really wants. Try this: "We have to be careful when naming this new product. It's got to reflect our brand accurately, and it's got to be memorable. For example, I want to avoid what happened to Disney when they opened their theme park in Europe. Michael Eisner tells the story . . ."

Source
Michael Eisner, *Work in Progress* (New York: Random House, 1998), p. 292.

Michael Eisner

THE WALT DISNEY COMPANY

The Worst They Can Say Is No

> Board Vote
> Being Asked
> Politicking

Talk about a potboiler. Throughout his tenure, Michael Eisner's relations with the Disney board were anything but run-of-the-mill. In discussing his quest to become CEO, he tells the story of the intense lobbying and constantly shifting alliances to get the votes he needed. Like a political cliffhanger, he tells of being one vote shy of the majority he needed to become Disney's head. Three votes remained undecided. All he needed to do was convince one of the three to vote his way and the corner office would be his. Eisner tells of how he went to meet with two of the undecided board members in Los Angeles. His ally, Frank Wells, would fly to Arizona to lobby the third person.

Eisner was worried that his efforts at pressing the flesh weren't working, and he tells of how he wasn't sure his two meetings had gone well. He called another trusted executive, only to hear the news that this individual had just gotten off the phone with Frank, who had met with the third board member. The vote was in the bag. Turns out this board member not only had been on Eisner's side all along, he was even willing to make the nominating speech at the board meeting the next day. Why had he been so curiously quiet up to this point? The issue for him was simple: He hadn't *been asked*.

Using This Anecdote

You can't always assume—either good or bad. We all know the joke that assuming makes a *you-know-what* out of you and me. Asking, often—but not always—leads to favorable results. In this case, it turns out this individual had been on Eisner's side all along; he was just waiting to be courted. How many opportunities have you missed by not actually asking? Try this: "Everyone, customers included, wants to be asked. They don't want people making assumptions about them either way. I'm reminded of a story Michael Eisner tells . . ."

Source

Michael Eisner, *Work in Progress* (New York: Random House, 1998), pp. 138–139.

Michael Eisner

THE WALT DISNEY COMPANY

Debits and Credits

> Accounting
> Humbling Experience
> Lack of Specialization
> Self-Improvement
> Spousal Competition

At least he knew numbers in the black were good. Michael Eisner—a highly successful businessman by any measure—tells the story of never having taken an accounting course when he was studying at New York University. As he was nearing the end of his contract at Paramount, he joked that it would be useful to finally take a course to better read a balance sheet properly. Although enthusiastic about this act of self-improvement, he wasn't about to face the course alone. He convinced his wife Jane to go along with him—as he says—"to share the pain." He says their kids enjoyed watching the two of them sweat out the course, taking time away from weekends to study and work on homework together.

As he saw it, he and his wife were as competitive as two high school seniors fighting for the honor of earning class valedictorian.

When it came time for the final exam, *both* felt the test was impossibly difficult. Jane was so sure she had flunked she refused to hand in her exam and failed anyhow. Eisner handed in his exam figuring that the test was so difficult, the professor would grade everyone on a curve. Indeed, that's exactly what happened. Eisner got an A. When they later reviewed Jane's answers, it turns out she would have gotten a higher grade if she'd only handed in her test. It didn't count, however. The lesson for him was better to try than forfeit.

Using This Anecdote

The fact that the CEO of a major corporation admits to never having taken an accounting course is probably story enough, but this cute anecdote of friendly spousal competition is a nice way to remind people that there's always room for self-improvement, or to show how important it is to bond with one's significant other. It also speaks to the fact that the CEO cannot possibly be an expert in every aspect of the business. Try this: "Not every CEO can be perfect in every part of the business. No one can, for that matter. Some are more right brain, others more left brain. Some see the big picture easily, while others prefer to dig deeper in the details. Take Michael Eisner, who's always been in creative enterprises . . ."

Source
Michael Eisner, *Work in Progress* (New York: Random House, 1998), pp. 106–107.

Michael Eisner

THE WALT DISNEY COMPANY

1 Percent Inspiration, 99 Percent Perspiration

> Creativity
> Weeding Out Ideas
> Odds Against Success

Success has many fathers. Failure's usually an orphan. When Michael Eisner was relatively new in his career, he developed a treatment for a television program that he readily admits was not ready for prime time. Later, when he actually headed a studio, he says he wanted to create an environment where people wouldn't be afraid to test new ideas. The key was not being penalized for the "wrong" idea. Instead of agonizing over decisions, there would be instant feedback—thumbs-up or adios . . . Ideas usually get neither better nor worse over time, Eisner reasoned. You know pretty quickly what's going to have potential—and what's best set aside.

Eisner says the weeding-out process can often be brutal. For example, for every idea a respected producer submits, at least ten possibilities have already been screened out beforehand. For every three ideas the network eventually hears, usually only one script is OK'd for development. For every three accepted scripts, one pilot is accepted.

For every three pilots made, only one goes on air. For every series that makes it on air, only one in four ends up returning for a second season. For every one that returns, only one in four becomes a true hit. And even then, only two or three times per decade does a show become a cultural phenomenon like *The Sopranos* or *Seinfeld*. By his own calculation, Eisner says that for even a seasoned producer, the odds of a modest success are around one in four thousand! But all it takes is *one* hit. "Persistence is as important as inspiration," he says.

Using This Anecdote

No matter what industry you're in, the odds of failure in trying something new are always better than the odds of success. That's business—that's life. Eisner's story is a good way to illustrate those odds using references everyone can identify with. Try this: "Let's be honest, the odds of failure are big. That's why it's more important than ever that we focus on improving those ideas at the front end. I'm reminded of a story by Michael Eisner who tells the odds of getting a show on television . . ."

Source
Michael Eisner, *Work in Progress* (New York: Random House, 1998), pp. 51–52.

Michael Eisner

THE WALT DISNEY COMPANY

Outward Bound for Execs

> Learning the Corporate Culture
> Creating Networks
> Learning by Doing

What happens when your CEO really *is* Mickey Mouse? Michael Eisner tells the story of how Walt Disney insisted on teaching by example. He was known, for example, to lean down and pick up trash at Disneyland. Years later, Eisner says he did the same—despite a bad back—at Walt Disney World. Executives not only have to talk the talk—they must walk the walk. That was part of the thinking behind an initiative called "Disney Dimensions," which Eisner calls a kind of "Hell Week" for executives to become more immersed in Disney culture. Part of the inspiration came from Eisner's own experience being a member of a college fraternity. Part also came from an existing program, Disney University.

Top brass had rarely attended this program in the past. But that soon changed as the nine-day program became required attendance. As in Outward Bound, executives were given hands-on experiences. For example, they would don character costumes like Mickey Mouse and Donald Duck at theme parks and walk around and mingle with guests. They were given briefings on details of the business, from the mundane, like how they peeled potatoes at their restaurants and how often restrooms were cleaned, to more important aspects of the business, like how movies and TV shows were selected for production. While at the beginning of the program many grumbled about how much time they were spending away from their work, by the end, most ended up loving the whole experience. Eisner says there was another benefit. Everyone ended up with "foxhole companions" whom they could rely on when they returned to their jobs. Camaraderie always widens and deepens networks in business.

Using This Anecdote

Many companies have training programs for their executives. But it's not every company that requires their top brass to walk around in cartoon costumes or learn how potatoes are peeled. Try this: "I know the next couple of days may seem like a drag to you, but believe me, it's important for you to understand our company's corporate culture. Disney, for example, has its own program . . ."

Source
Michael Eisner, *Work in Progress* (New York: Random House, 1998), pp. 236–237.

Larry Ellison

ORACLE

Irrational Exuberance

> Bubble Economics
> Hype
> Internet Boom
> Valuation

Call it the Zeitgeist of the digital age. The Internet bubble of the late 1990s spawned some crazy ideas: everything from online guitar lessons to home kitty litter delivery, and many more too numerous to mention here. Oracle founder Larry Ellison says he and some friends tried to test just how far the euphoria for this newfound technology really went. He says at the height of the bubble he and a group of friends started a website called HeyIdiot.com. But wait, it gets better . . . They made nothing. They did nothing. Their sole activity was selling stock in, well, *themselves*. Their plan was to then auction off HeyIdiot.com to the highest bidder.

Much to Ellison's surprise, some people actually fell for their tongue-in-cheek ruse. He says some even sent emails saying the site wasn't working and asking when it would be back up. Others said they were trying to buy the stock but nothing was happening. They even got a call from someone who was interested in buying the website's name. According to Ellison, this person thought the site "was worth hundreds of thousands of dollars. More madness." Not the first time a bubble produced irrational exuberance and, unfortunately, not the last.

Using This Anecdote

The legendary circus impresario P. T. Barnum once said there's a sucker born every minute. Generations later, he has yet to be proven wrong. Ellison's example of irrational exuberance in the midst of an economic bubble is a hilarious anecdote of just how far people will go if they believe what they want to believe. Try this: "I know there's a lot of pressure for us to invest in what looks like a growing market, but we should be cognizant of what can also be a bubble about to burst. We all remember the tech bubble, right? Oracle's Larry Ellison tells a great story . . ."

Source

Stephen Randall, ed., *The Playboy Interviews: Movers and Shakers* (Milwaukie, OR: M Press, 2007), pp. 435–436.

Larry Ellison

ORACLE

What Box?

> Challenging Conventional Wisdom
> Innovation
> Risk
> Succeeding in Business

For Larry Ellison, it really is hip to be square. He says he actually got ahead in business by challenging the current conventional wisdom. Even in small matters like clothes. Though he was someone who made it big in Silicon Valley, where T-shirts and jeans are de rigueur in board meetings, he wore suits instead. His nonconformity may have hurt him socially, but it was key to his success in business, he says. His belief? You can't innovate by copying. "The only way you can succeed in business big-time is to find places where conventional wisdom is wrong—to find errors in the fashion." Like Galileo challenging the conventional wisdom that the sun revolves around the earth. It may get you into trouble, it may make you enemies, but it's ultimately all the more rewarding when you're proven right.

Ellison says that at least once every five years you have to find that error in the conventional wisdom and do things differently—otherwise you're not truly innovating. For example, he made Oracle the only company to believe that a relational database—which matches data together by finding common characteristics—could be commercialized. He says IBM even wrote a white paper on the subject, but Oracle was the first to market. He also made Oracle the first company to base all of its software on the Internet. "Everyone said we were crazy." Was it an arrogant decision? Probably. Did it entail huge risk? Yes. But "thinking outside the box is tough because the box has very strong walls, floor, and ceiling. But it's the only way to win big."

Using This Anecdote

Risk and innovation go hand in hand. True innovators are often a lonely lot—until the conventional wisdom shifts their way. Then they're seen as having been ahead of their time, at least until the conventional wisdom shifts again. And shift it will. Try this: "It may seem like we're swimming upstream and getting nowhere, but I want to remind everybody that innovation only comes with taking risks. Larry Ellison at Oracle talks a lot about challenging conventional wisdom . . ."

Source
Stephen Randall, ed., *The Playboy Interviews: Movers and Shakers* (Milwaukie, OR: M Press, 2007), pp. 448–449.

Larry Ellison

ORACLE

All You Need Is Love

> Adoption
> Family
> Respect vs. Love

Like Steve Jobs, Larry Ellison was an adopted child. His mother gave him to an aunt and uncle living in a different city when he was only nine months old. He never knew his birth father and only met his birth mother when he was in his late forties. He tells a story of when he was a teenager and talking with his sister, who would later become a psychologist. She asked him what was more important: to be loved or respected? He answered quickly saying it was more important to be respected. She told him he was wrong. After initially getting annoyed, he paused and thought about it longer. He then told her he still thought it was more important to be respected than loved. "We've got to find that someplace in our lives," he says.

But then he changed his mind. He adds that his place is with his adoptive family, where the love his adopted parents showed him trumped genes. He says he realized that even after he met his biological family. "I didn't belong to them," he says. "I belonged to the family that raised me. It eliminated all ambiguity."

Using This Anecdote

While it may be more important to be respected in business, as well-rounded individuals we also need more than just respect. Try this: "Work-life balance is critical for each of us. The fact is the rules of the workplace don't apply at home. I'm reminded of a revealing story Larry Ellison tells of when he was younger . . ."

Source
Stephen Randall, ed., *The Playboy Interviews: Movers and Shakers* (Milwaukie, OR: M Press, 2007), pp. 447–448.

Carly Fiorina

HEWLETT-PACKARD

Taking on the Empty Suits

> Fairness
> Judging Performance
> Career Risks

Carly Fiorina faced tough odds succeeding in a male-dominated business. She tells the story of how some aspiring managers at a major telecom company where she had worked prior to joining HP would get ahead more by schmoozing and looking the part than by actually *being* the part. She calls them "42-longs," after the suit size for individuals who were just that—empty suits. She says the managers there would conduct annual performance reviews, rating and ranking subordinates. All too often, however, how long you'd been with the company or how well liked you were trumped actual achievement. She says a lot of horse trading went on one year among managers rating their direct reports. She had been rated highly because of her stellar performance, but ranked lower than she should have been because another manager said his direct report didn't get promoted last year. His reasoning: It was now the other person's turn to advance; Fiorina should wait until next year.

In an underhanded move, the manager made up tales about Fiorina saying that when she worked for him, she took credit for other people's work. It wasn't even remotely true. In fact, she had never even worked with this person! When she later learned of the deception, she confronted him. She eventually got him to admit in front of the others that he had fibbed. Shaking and trembling after leaving the meeting, she worried that she had just killed a promising career. The next day, however, the now remorseful manager apologized to her. In confronting the manager, Fiorina had taken a big career risk—but fair's fair. Sometimes you have to stand your ground, even when confronting those above you. She writes that it was also the first time she had experienced how personal power could triumph over positional power.

Using This Anecdote

Fiorina took a big risk in confronting an individual who was more interested in playing office politics than in being fair to deserving high achievers. This story is especially appropriate when talking about performance reviews and the need to put company interests over personal friendships. Try this: "We need fairness and objectivity in how we judge performance at this company. I sure don't want to see a situation similar to what Carly Fiorina faced early in her career . . ."

Source
Carly Fiorina, *Tough Choices* (New York: Portfolio, 2006), pp. 44–45.

Carly Fiorina

HEWLETT-PACKARD

Changing the World

> Developing World
> Empowerment
> Leadership
> Technological Change

Borders can't keep talent hidden forever these days. Carly Fiorina tells the story of a rural community in South Africa called Mogalakwena, where HP had committed itself to help with the community's development using cutting-edge technology. They were already confidently using the company's technology in libraries, schools, and health clinics. Some three thousand people—ranging in age from thirteen to seventy-four—had graduated from the PC literacy courses they sponsored. She said she saw many of them busy applying their newly learned skills on long-distance learning and other pursuits.

She tells the story of meeting someone named Sali George Missinga. Sali had been an uneducated and impoverished denizen of Mogalakwena who had been hired by HP to move boxes of equipment to various community centers. Simple work, but Sali had a very curious mind. After watching the equipment in use, he asked the technicians to show him how to use it. A year later, Sali became the technical expert they'd send to do installations. Talking with the young man, Fiorina said that she would mention his story when she spoke later with then South African president Thabo Mbeki. When she gave a speech later that day, she asked Sali to come onstage. He did. He then gave an emotional speech about how technology had transformed his life and empowered him to pursue a career he never thought possible. Moved by Sali's story, the South African president told him before the crowd: "Young man, I'm going to send you to college!" As Fiorina says, "In the twenty-first century, for the first time in human history, anyone can lead."

Using This Anecdote

For all the hype about how technology can change lives, it's easy to forget that some lives can be changed profoundly—particularly for those possessing none of the advantages of modern society. No, not everyone gets a public promise from the leader of their country to pay for their college education, but the point about empowerment is clear enough. Try this: "We hear a lot about the latest apps improving our lives or the latest gadget helping us communicate faster, etc. But amid all our abundance, we forget how much of the rest of the world lives and we forget how profoundly their lives can change as well . . ."

Source
Carly Fiorina, *Tough Choices* (New York: Portfolio, 2006), pp. 270–271.

Malcolm Forbes

FORBES

Born to Be Wild

> Brainstorming
> Focus
> Different Perspective
> Trying Something New

Maybe you can teach an old dog new tricks. The late publisher Malcolm Forbes started two of his favorite hobbies, ballooning and motorcycling, relatively late in life. He says he was fifty—old enough to qualify for AARP membership!—when he first tried riding a motorcycle. One of his chauffeurs had apparently wanted to buy one and asked Forbes if he could borrow the money from him. Forbes could clearly afford to front him the money, but still said no. He tried to talk the man out of buying a motorcycle, saying it was too dangerous. His chauffeur went ahead and bought one anyhow. One day, he took Forbes for a ride and the publisher was hooked. Forbes then started buying and selling his own, and it became a passion of his.

Forbes says he loved the experience of riding because it exposes you to the elements, heightens your senses, and allows you to concentrate better and focus on issues that you likely would be distracted thinking about at the office. For him, it allowed him to really brain-storm business challenges. "The one problem," he said, "is that it's rather difficult to jot down your notes on a notepad at seventy miles an hour, so the terrific new ideas you get are usually gone with the wind by the time you stop, but some of them stay." He hints that some of the people who worked for him may actually have preferred it that way because they knew he was less likely to flood them with ideas precisely because he couldn't write them down at seventy miles an hour!

Using This Anecdote

We all have different ways of teasing out our best ideas. For some it's total silence and pure focus. For others, it's calming music. For Malcolm Forbes, it was pushing the speed limit on a Harley roaring down the highway. Whatever works to get the creative juices flowing and get your mind focused on the task at hand. Try this: "I know everyone approaches brainstorming differently. Everyone has their own method. In my case, I do it a lot differently than Malcolm Forbes . . ."

Source
Stephen Randall, ed., *The Playboy Interviews: Movers and Shakers* (Milwaukie, OR: M Press, 2007), p. 470.

Malcolm Forbes

FORBES

Change

> Caution
> Putting Money to Work
> Risk

Since he is someone who enjoys the risky sports of motorcycling and ballooning, it should come as no surprise that Malcolm Forbes says the biggest risk in life—and business—is too much caution. Being totally risk averse is a formula for failure in business.

He says that when businesses reach a point where they say, "This is how we've always done it and we'll keep doing it that way," that's when the momentum gets lost and companies lose their way. "Safety doesn't lie in that," he says. "Just ask the Pennsylvania Railroad and the people who owned Erie Canal bonds." Forbes adds that safety doesn't lie in stashing or holding on to money. "Moving it," he says, "putting it to work, is safety."

Using This Anecdote

In what is less a story than a warning, Forbes's point is well taken. Companies that get complacent in their ways ultimately put themselves in danger. Try this: "If we keep relying on the old way of doing things, we will never grow. Malcolm Forbes says safety lies in putting money to work. He's right . . ."

Source
Stephen Randall, ed., *The Playboy Interviews: Movers and Shakers* (Milwaukie, OR: M Press, 2007), p. 481.

Bill Gates

MICROSOFT

Getting A's

> Family Competition
> External Event
> Incentive

Sibling rivalry can have some amazing side effects. When he was company chairman, Microsoft founder Bill Gates was known for being ruthlessly competitive. He says that when he was growing up his parents were major influences on his and his sister's lives. Their grandparents also had an influence, actively encouraging them to read at an early age and get good grades. They were also told about adult challenges early on, the assumption being that they would understand and appreciate the advice even at their young age.

Gates says he was often competing against his sister, who is two years older. He tells the story of how both were rewarded with 25 cents each time they got an A on their report card. He says there was a long stretch where he was getting terrible grades and his sister was collecting one A after another. The tables turned when Bill was in the eighth grade, however. It was at that time that his sister starting noticing boys, and she apparently didn't get the grades she used to after that. According to Gates, it was at this point that his grade point average went from a 2.2 to a 4.0 during the summer because he knew he could do it and didn't want people thinking he was below par academically.

Using This Anecdote

While some of Gates's competitors may now wish his sister had never discovered boys, this anecdote can help illustrate the early roots of a person's competitive nature, or how external events can motivate people to change. Try this: "Sometimes the potential is always there, but it takes an outside event to trigger motivation. There's a funny story Bill Gates tells . . ."

Source

Stephen Randall, ed., *The Playboy Interviews: Movers and Shakers* (Milwaukie, OR: M Press, 2007), pp. 466–467.

Bill Gates

MICROSOFT

The Vision Thing

> Addressing Your Audience
> Internal vs. External Communications
> Messaging
> Tagline

Not all taglines are created equal. Bill Gates tells the story of when one of Microsoft's early taglines appeared in an article written about the company in the late 1970s. The article mentioned that the company's vision was to have "A computer on every desk and in every home . . ." Remember, at that time, computers were usually enormous and incredibly expensive, most often used by large companies that could afford them. At the same time, the smaller models that would become the precursors of today's smaller desktops, laptops, and handheld devices were largely confined to a very small number of hobbyists. These models, too, were out of range for the average consumer. Gates even says that Ken Olsen—the former head of Digital Equipment, the company that made the computer Gates grew up with—thought the idea of people wanting a computer at home was way off base.

When talking about the company's vision internally, however,

Gates would say, "A computer on every desk and in every home . . . *running Microsoft software.*" In front of an external audience, he'd leave the last part out, but if he were speaking internally at Microsoft, the last part definitely stayed. It depended on the audience. You can have a vision, but that vision is often going to mean different things to different people.

Using This Anecdote

A company's name is one thing. A description of that company's vision is a completely different matter and can be vital for clear communications. For example, a tagline helps not only the people working for you but also the rest of the world understand what your business is all about. It can be a rallying cry for your troops. Try this: "When we launch this new campaign, it's important that we understand our audiences. Different stakeholders will see it from different angles. I'm reminded of a story Bill Gates tells from early in Microsoft's history . . ."

Source
Academy of Achievement, "Software Architect of the Computer Age," Seattle, Washington, March 17, 2010: www.achievement.org/autodoc/page/gat0int-1.

Bill Gates

MICROSOFT

It Costs How Much?

> Ahead of the Curve
> Creating Opportunities
> Moving Quickly
> Timing

It started with sticker shock. Some forty years ago, the cost of a computer was astronomical. According to Bill Gates, minicomputers in the early 1970s were averaging between $10,000 and $200,000! Far out of range for the typical consumer. Even out of range for many businesses! Bill Gates tells the story of how he and Microsoft's cofounder, Paul Allen, saw an obscure article about a microprocessor Intel was developing called the 4004. Both knew that processing ability was increasing exponentially, so it was only a matter of time before the price would come down.

By 1973, the 8080 chip had been introduced. Gates and Allen began to think, "OK, this is far better than most of these minicomputers. Someone's going to take that chip and do something wild." In late 1974, *Popular Electronics* ran its now famous cover piece on the Altair, a computer kit for hobbyists. Both Gates and Allen immediately realized that what they had predicted was coming true. With Gates still at Harvard and Allen at Washington State, the two decided to contact the manufacturer in New Mexico and ask them if they could do the software for their new machine. The pitch worked. The budding entrepreneurs soon started work on a program for the computer—and they didn't even have an actual computer at hand! They went back and forth with the company asking numerous questions. Gates says the customer was thinking, "You guys may not be flaky, because you're the first ones to actually ask that question." He says it took them six weeks to write the program. With only four kilobytes of memory, he says it was "probably the most fun piece of software I ever wrote."

Using This Anecdote

Timing's critical—and not just for comedians. It can spell the difference between success and failure in business, too. Gates and Allen were keeping up with the bleeding-edge trends in the industry while waiting for the right moment to act. Any earlier wouldn't have made sense. Any later might have meant someone else running with the idea. Try this: "They say there's no such thing as luck. What many consider luck is actually the point at which preparation meets opportunity. We have to do both—prepare *and* create opportunities. I'm reminded of a story Bill Gates tells . . ."

Source

Academy of Achievement, "Software Architect of the Computer Age," Seattle, Washington, March 17, 2010: www.achievement.org/autodoc/page/gat0int-1.

Bill Gates

MICROSOFT

"Good Morning, Allen and Gates . . ."

> Anticipation of Growth
> Branding
> Naming a Company

What's in a name? A lot, actually. Microsoft cofounders Bill Gates and Paul Allen had been planning on starting a company for quite some time. They had already started working with their first major customer, MITS in Albuquerque, New Mexico, doing the software for their computer, the Altair. Still students, the duo had already been trying out different names for the company they knew they would eventually found.

When they were much younger—still kids—they had experimented with all kinds of company names. One obvious choice was "Allen & Gates." It sounded OK at the time, but they quickly realized it projected the wrong image. They wanted to start a company on the technological cutting edge, not a law firm! Gates says that since they were the first to do microcomputer software, the choice of naming the company "Microsoft" seemed obvious "and we thought it was a cool term." He says they both knew the name would also have longevity, which was important given their obviously ambitious plans. They thought at the time: "Hey, we're going to have a big company, so we'll have a [big-sounding] company name. So 'Microsoft' was a very natural choice."

Using This Anecdote

Shakespeare may have said that a rose by any other name would smell as sweet, but then again, Shakespeare was never exactly called upon to name a company. A name needs to sound and feel right, not to mention fit a brand image. Even naming an initiative within an existing company can affect whether it's accepted or not. Who's going to follow the banner of "Increase Revenue by 12%!" Snore. "Fit to Win" sounds a lot better. Try this: "How we name this initiative is critical for its success. For example, how many people here have used software from a company called Allen & Gates? Nobody, of course. That was one of the early names rejected by the company that would go on to become Microsoft. Gates tells the story . . ."

Source
Academy of Achievement, "Software Architect of the Computer Age," Seattle, Washington, March 17, 2010: www.achievement.org/autodoc/page/gat0int-1.

Carl Gerstacker

THE DOW CHEMICAL COMPANY

If You Can't Beat 'Em . . .

> Living with Confrontation
> Publicity
> Recruiting

What's worse than being talked about? *Not* being talked about. Carl Gerstacker's tenure as chairman of Dow Chemical coincided with the Vietnam War during the 1960s—a period of political and social upheaval for the United States. Dow had been making napalm—a chemical used in the war to clear the jungle—often with devastating effects. Protests followed company representatives, as did people who supported the company's position. Gerstacker was reportedly even on the receiving end of death threats. He told the story of a Dow recruiter who went to a California school to seek out potential new hires.

He said students were lined up in the hallway waiting to see the recruiter for jobs with Dow—or to express their opposition to the company. In the booth next to him was a recruiter for Standard of California—the precursor of today's Chevron. No one was lined up to see him. The poor fellow did some paperwork, looked around, but no one approached his booth. Frustrated that Dow was overflowing while he had no students to speak of, the Standard recruiter stood up, went out into the hallway, and loudly announced, "Gentlemen, I think you ought to know that we at Standard of California supply the gasoline to Dow Chemical that it uses to make napalm. Now, wouldn't some of you like to interview with me?"

Using This Anecdote

Sometimes companies—rightly or wrongly—are on the receiving end of public criticism. This story neatly illustrates the old rule that publicity of any kind—even bad publicity—is better than none at all. Try this: "I know when we go out in public we're sometimes confronted by individuals opposed to us. That's fine, we live in a democracy. But remember, even bad attention can sometimes work in our favor. The late chairman of Dow Chemical, Carl Gerstacker, told the story . . ."

Source
E. N. Brandt, *Chairman of the Board* (East Lansing, MI: Michigan State University Press, 2003), p. 103.

Carl Gerstacker

THE DOW CHEMICAL COMPANY

In the Beginning . . .

> Off-Color Joke
> Traveling to Different Cities
> Speech Opener

Not your typical speech opener these days, but still funny. Unquestionably part of the pre–politically correct era, Dow Chemical chairman Carl Gerstacker was fond of repeating variations on the same joke to different cities he'd travel to across the country. He called it the "Mabel joke." He would tell audiences that as soon as he arrived late in the city he was traveling to (Chicago, Los Angeles, Pittsburgh, or wherever), he would usually be in no mood to go to sleep right away. Bored and looking for something to read, he once pulled out a copy of the Gideon's Bible in the nightstand.

He opened it up to the first page and saw that someone had written, "If you're having trouble sleeping, try reading the 23rd Psalm." He thought to himself how kind it was to offer such friendly advice, so he turned to that page. On the page with the 23rd Psalm, the same person had written that if you're still having trouble sleeping, go to the thirteenth chapter of II Corinthians. And so on. This went on for several pages, and Gerstacker thought to himself, "Wow, what nice people here, how considerate they are to travelers here!" Finally he turned to the next page as instructed, and in completely different handwriting someone had written: "And if you're still having trouble, hi there, my name is Mabel, and if you call me at 123-4567, I'll come right over . . ."

Using This Anecdote

Obviously more a relic of the *Mad Men* era—or earlier—Gerstacker says this joke always got a laugh when he told it. Be sure, however, that the audience you're addressing will get the humor and not be offended. Try this: "I've heard people in this city are especially friendly, and I've seen it myself. I'm reminded of a story by the former chair of Dow Chemical, who used to travel to other cities and made a similar observation . . ."

Source
E. N. Brandt, *Chairman of the Board* (East Lansing, MI: Michigan State University Press, 2003), p. 85.

Carl Gerstacker

THE DOW CHEMICAL COMPANY

So What's Your Question?

> Protests
> Questioning Management
> Shareholders' Meeting

Free speech is a cornerstone of democracy—but patience isn't limit-less. Protests against Dow Chemical's involvement with supplying napalm spread to the company's annual shareholders' meeting. Pro-testors had gained access to the meeting one year and proceeded to use the forum as a platform for speeches. Although Gerstacker com-pletely respected opponents' right to free speech, he also understood that the never-ending speeches were preventing business from getting done. One by one, the student protesters would approach the micro-phone and start what were more often rambling lectures than true questions. Gerstacker himself would patiently answer each question later, saying his biggest problem was not really the students—who had a right to be there—but restraining employees and shareholders who felt the students had made their point and should either behave for the rest of the meeting or be kicked out!

The experience resulted in what would later be called "Gerstacker's

Rule." If it takes more than five minutes to ask a question, it's not a question, it's a speech. Same for the answer. If it takes more than five minutes to answer a question, it's not an answer, it's also a speech. In either case at Dow meetings, if the time limit passed, the individual would be gaveled down. The limit was subsequently scaled down to three minutes. Gerstacker would later say that he was careful to distinguish between two different types of students. He would engage those interested in *real* debate, usually not the loudest, whose main goal—at least at the time—appeared to be shutting everything down.

Using This Anecdote

Not every company faces protests—but some do. It's a normal part of living in a free society. But even in a free society, there should be agreed-upon rules of engagement. "Gerstacker's Rule" of no more than a few minutes to ask your question is probably a good rule of thumb for a public session, where questions are more for public consumption than a serious effort to start a dialogue. Try this: "I know this is a controversial topic and I'd be happy to take questions now, but I'd like to invoke the 'three-minute rule' that Dow Chemical follows . . ."

Source

E. N. Brandt, *Chairman of the Board* (East Lansing, MI: Michigan State University Press, 2003), pp. 99–100.

Carl Gerstacker

THE DOW CHEMICAL COMPANY

You Used First-Class Postage?

> Former Chairmen
> Company Image
> Shareholder Concerns
> Thriftiness

Perception matters, even if it's only over a few cents. Years after he retired, Dow Chemical chair Carl Gerstacker called the company's then CFO Robert Keil. The call was from Gerstacker not as a former chairman, but instead as a shareholder in the company. He had read Dow's most recent annual report and noticed that the president's message this year mentioned what was described as a "great cost savings program" the company was launching.

Gerstacker then quizzed the CFO as to why Dow—in light of this great cost savings program—spent $1.39 per copy to send the annual report in a first-class envelope. The former CEO said that he had already checked with the post office and found out that "about 20 cents would have done the job without the envelope." Red-faced, Keil said it was clearly a mistake he would look into. He then instructed his staff to report back to Gerstacker on "a handwritten note on used scratch paper, delivered by the cheapest means possible."

Using This Anecdote

Don't think small details—especially contradictions—go unnoticed. If something doesn't jibe with your messaging, or you appear to be talking the talk but not walking the walk, be ready. Someone will notice, perhaps someone with a lot of pull. Try this: "We have to be careful we're consistent here. We can't say one thing and then find out that somewhere we're actually doing the polar opposite. I'm reminded of a story about a former CEO . . ."

Source
E. N. Brandt, *Chairman of the Board* (East Lansing, MI: Michigan State University Press, 2003), p. 158.

> Information Overload
> Analysis Paralysis
> Death by PowerPoint

Sometimes the best way to communicate is the simplest way possible: Forget the high-tech distractions—just get up and speak! Lou Gerstner tells the story of an important meeting he had not long after becoming IBM's CEO. It was with the team heading IBM's then faltering mainframe business. It was an important session for all involved because if that business continued to perform below expectations, the fate of the entire company could hang in the balance.

At that time, company meetings were often run using a presentation system that was essentially a forerunner of PowerPoint, known in IBM vernacular at the time as "foils." The person presenting knew his stuff but was essentially repeating minute details already on the foil. By the time the presenter got to the second slide, Gerstner had stood up, walked over to the projector, and—to the surprise of everyone in the room—turned it off! The screen went blank. The audience sat for a moment in stunned silence, until Gerstner turned to the presenting

IBM employee and said as politely as he could, "Let's just talk about your business." And they did. News of the incident spread like wildfire throughout the company via emails that crisscrossed multiple time zones. The point was clear, though. The chairman wanted a *real* discussion of the challenges that division faced, not a slide show. Gerstner then credits the honest discussion that followed with later helping make a mission-critical decision for the business. It wouldn't have happened, though, if Gerstner hadn't challenged the status quo and asked for clarity.

Using This Anecdote

Tell your story as simply as possible. It's too easy to hide behind content-laden presentations. Tell your story in the most compelling way and use visuals to back it up, not as the main event. If your company is suffering from death by PowerPoint, start by saying, "I want to use as few slides today as possible so we can have a real dialogue, something we need more of here. It reminds me of a story about IBM . . ."

Source
Louis V. Gerstner, *Who Says Elephants Can't Dance?* (New York: Harper-Collins, 2002), pp. 42–43.

Lou Gerstner

IBM

Remember Who's the Boss

> Global Communications
> Asserting Control from the Top
> Sabotaging Progress
> Employees

One of the biggest challenges Lou Gerstner faced early after taking over the helm at IBM in 1993 was restructuring a company that often consisted of fiefdoms of employees jealously guarding their turf. His goal? Turn it into a truly global, transparent, customer-centric organization. No easy task. As an outsider trying to assert control from the top, Gerstner was repeatedly told that he would sink Big Blue if he moved forward too aggressively. He moved ahead anyway, only to often find resistance from below. He recounts the story of how during a trip to Europe he accidentally found out that employees there were not receiving his global, company-wide emails, which he had been using to outline his vision of where he wanted the company to go. How could they understand the changes he was trying to make back at headquarters if they weren't receiving his messages in the first place?

When he asked the head of European operations why IBM's

European employees were not receiving his messages, the individual said Gerstner's emails were not appropriate for *his* employees in Europe. Plus, they were hard to translate. Gerstner later summoned this individual to the headquarters in the United States. He firmly told him that *all* employees belonged to IBM and he was to stop interfering with company-wide communications sent from the global CEO's office. Period. The executive sheepishly agreed but never fully got on board and later left the company. Not a pleasant experience, but necessary to assert control.

Using This Anecdote

Sometimes you have to remind people—subtly, or not so subtly—of exactly who signs the paychecks. Sabotaging efforts from the headquarters is done at one's peril, especially when it comes to something as important to the CEO as all-company messages were in this example from Lou Gerstner. Try this: "We need to communicate our vision throughout the entire company, to all employees, from the top down. People throughout the organization are looking to senior management for leadership. They're looking for a clear signal as to which direction the company is headed. They're looking to us. I'm reminded of a story about Lou Gerstner at IBM . . ."

Source

Louis V. Gerstner, *Who Says Elephants Can't Dance?* (New York: Harper-Collins, 2002), p. 87.

Lou Gerstner

IBM

Three Simple Words

> Communication
> Corporate Culture Change
> Leadership Competencies
> Message Simplification
> Performance Commitment

Call it IBM's "sophomore slump." A few years after Lou Gerstner launched a major corporate cultural transformation at IBM in the mid-1990s, moving away from countless fiefdoms that jealously guarded their territory and increasingly toward a more unified, customer-centric organization, he saw his efforts start to stall. He says the setback was far from unexpected but still needed to be addressed. Many employees were buying into the cultural changes begun under Gerstner, but in some cases it often remained an intellectual exercise: Think the new culture, act the old. As Gerstner aptly puts it, "Since people don't do what you *ex*pect, but what you *in*spect, I needed to create a way to measure results."

Gerstner says he needed to simplify his message in order to make the change more real, more impactful. He recalls a conversation he had with a colleague who had actually added up all the things Gerstner had expected him to focus on. The list came to about two dozen. "I can't do it," he told Gerstner. "I'm not that good. What do you really want people to do?" Gerstner thought for a second and told him the absolute essence of his message: "Win, execute, and team." Those three would define the new culture, but do so with substance. "Win" meant they had to see the world as competitive. The opponent was out to eat your lunch. "Execute" meant focusing on speed and discipline. No more analysis paralysis. Move quickly, move decisively. "Team" was the simplest of all. Act as one IBM. Period. The three eventually became part of IBM's annual planning, and employees were required to list the actions they were going to take in the year ahead to fulfill those commitments. These weren't empty promises, either. Success or failure in these areas determined merit and variable pay.

Using This Anecdote

IBM wanted to develop leaders, but its message was unfocused. A chance encounter with an employee forced Gerstner to boil his message down to its essence. This was exactly the focus the company needed to continue its culture change and make sure no momentum was lost. Try this: "Companies need goals with vision they can understand instead of laundry lists of to-do items they know they'll never achieve. There's a lot to be said for keeping our messages simple so our managers not only know what's expected but also have realistic expectations when it comes to achieving those goals. Lou Gerstner tells the story of . . ."

Source

Louis V. Gerstner, *Who Says Elephants Can't Dance?* (New York: HarperCollins, 2002), p. 87.

Lou Gerstner

IBM

I Can Get You a Good Deal on a Bridge in Brooklyn . . .

> Skepticism
> Asking the Right Questions
> Deals That Sound Too Good to Be True

Never underestimate the value of a good defense—or an ounce of skepticism. Looking back on his career, former CEO Lou Gerstner confesses that much of his success at IBM was due not just to the deals he did—but to the deals he *didn't* do. He says this was especially true with many of the opportunities presented to him by investment banks promising the stars and the moon but glossing over critical facts. One episode in particular stands out. He tells the story of a banker who approached him with a plan for IBM to acquire a major computer manufacturer. It sounded great. The market would love it! The transaction's executive summary predicted that with the acquisition of this company, IBM's stock price would go through the roof for years to come. Who could object to that?

Gerstner was skeptical, though. He closely scrutinized the appendix where the forecasts were spelled out in detail. To his surprise, he found that IBM's profits would actually be wiped out if they went ahead with the deal. He then asked his CFO to question the banker about this. The banker told the CFO that wouldn't matter to the investment community; they should just go ahead anyhow. If only it were that simple! No deal. It's the CEO's job to be hard-nosed and critical about these matters because, statistically, most mergers fail. Asking the right questions can help prevent making a mistake that could easily erase all your other accomplishments. If you're not watching the bottom line, who is?

Using This Anecdote

The devil is often in the details, especially when acquisitions might look good on paper but just don't feel right. This story illustrates the point that you need to ask critical questions and play the role of devil's advocate, especially when something sounds too good to be true (it often is). Try this: "Prudence pays—or, more often than not, at least stops you from losing money. It's always a good idea to ask critical questions especially when we're being asked to engage in a project where more than your usual share of risk may be involved. That reminds me of a story at IBM where some critical questions kept them from making what could have been a big mistake . . ."

Source

Louis V. Gerstner, *Who Says Elephants Can't Dance?* (New York: Harper-Collins, 2002), p. 221.

Lou Gerstner

IBM

This Guy Wants to Eat Your Lunch!

> Firing Up the Troops
> Passion Against the Competition
> Personalizing the Argument
> Sales

First impressions count. Lou Gerstner wanted his first meeting with more than four hundred of the company's senior management to be a real barn burner. He tells the story of how he needed to show he was going to be different from his predecessor. He also needed to instill a sense of urgency among employees to turn things around and focus on beating the competition instead of on internal conflict. The situation was indeed dire. Big Blue had lost about half its market share in an industry that was growing. It was ranked poorly in customer satisfaction surveys—sometimes losing even to companies that didn't exist anymore!

Gerstner decided to try something IBM was not used to—he made it personal. His presentation showed pictures of competing CEOs and the negative comments they were saying about IBM, mocking Big Blue's fall from grace. Gerstner said everyone in the room had to focus on the competition, not intellectually, but viscerally. He added that since he had started, he had received thousands of emails from employees who spoke about the passion they felt for IBM. But none spoke of any passion against the competition. Gerstner said they had to feel that competitive pressure, to beat the other guy, in their guts, not their heads. He said they should view it as if the competition were coming into their homes and robbing their kids' and their grandkids' college funds—that's how they had to mentally prepare themselves for battle. The talk appeared to work. The message of the new CEO was now clear: Gerstner was not happy with the status quo, and people had better start feeling some fire in their guts if they wanted to be around for much longer.

Using This Anecdote

When companies focus too much on internal matters—and not enough on beating the competition—even big companies like IBM can stumble. Try this: "We face a tough situation here. When Lou Gerstner started at IBM, he also faced a tremendous challenge. His company lacked the will to fight . . ." If your company is in a similar situation and you have the opportunity to make a similar speech, consider using the same technique as Gerstner. When channeled properly, this can be a strong motivator for people.

Source
Louis V. Gerstner, *Who Says Elephants Can't Dance?* (New York: Harper-Collins, 2002), pp. 203–207.

Andy Grove

INTEL

It's Spelled G-r-o-v-e

> Becoming an American
> Immigrants
> Fitting In

Talk about beating the odds. Former Intel CEO and chairman Andy Grove, a Hungarian immigrant, went through more than his share of adversity. He survived World War II as a child, came of age under a communist regime, and managed to rise to the top of one of America's most well-known companies in a fiercely competitive industry. Not long after he arrived in the United States, green card in hand, his future looked bright except for one thing: his name. He liked being called "Andy," which fit perfectly. But his family name, Grof, was often mispronounced as "Gruff." Not exactly the image he wanted to project.

Then Grove learned from friends about another Hungarian who had Americanized his name so the pronunciation in English came closer to the Hungarian original. Grof decided he would try that with his name. At first, he tried to anglicize his name by putting an "e" at the end to make "Grofe." A friend who read the name said it looked like "Gro-fay." Not quite. He then wrote down "Grove" and tried it out on an American friend, who said, "Oh, that's how you say it." Perfect. All he had to do was wait to become a citizen: At that point, he could make a formal name change. In the meantime, he was told to be consistent about using his new name. After making the choice, he says he wrote to his parents, concluding the letter with the following: "From your son Andy, whose name will soon be Grove . . ."

Using This Anecdote

America's a nation of immigrants. Andy Grove's story about his path from adversity to success is an inspirational one. In showing his effort to fit into a new adopted land, the story of his search for just the right Americanized version of his name is a good one to remind people that the American dream is alive and well. Try this: "Sometimes you just have to be flexible until you find the right solution, especially if you're adapting to new circumstances. I'm reminded of a story Andy Grove tells . . ."

Source
Andrew S. Grove, *Swimming Across* (New York: Warner Books, 2001), pp. 284–285.

Andy Grove

INTEL

Walk Out the Door and Come Back In

> Brutal Competition
> Exiting a Business
> Leadership
> Pricing

It seems every decade has its competitor bogeyman. It's easy to forget, but in the 1980s, Japan was challenging U.S. predominance in many markets, not the least of which was the semiconductor business. It took time, but by 1985, Japan eventually beat the United States in worldwide market share. Before then, Grove recounts stories of how people would visit Japan, only to come back with alarming stories of how Japanese companies had entire floors dedicated to memory chip R&D. One floor, for example, would be R&D for 16K chips, another for 64K, another for 256K, and so on. Add that to what seemed like Japanese competitors' endless access to capital, and for a relatively "smaller" company like Intel, this was pretty scary stuff.

In one incident, Intel got access to a memo that had been sent to the sales force of a Japanese competitor. In part, it read: "Win the 10% rule . . . Find AMD and Intel sockets . . . quote 10% below their price . . . If they require, go 10% AGAIN . . . Don't quit until you WIN." By the middle of 1985, the situation was becoming untenable. No matter what Intel did, it seemed their Japanese competitors had them beat on price, quality, and selection. The mood throughout the company was glum. There were endless internal debates, and the situation only worsened with time. Grove then met with Intel's legendary chairman, Gordon Moore. He asked Moore a hypothetical question. If the two of them were fired and the board brought in a new CEO, what would that new CEO do? Moore didn't hesitate. The new CEO would get out of the memory business. Grove says he was numb at Moore's answer. He thought about it for a second, and said, "Why shouldn't you and I walk out the door, come back, and do it ourselves?" And that's exactly what happened—they literally and figuratively walked out the door and came back determined to make the changes necessary to survive.

Using This Anecdote

Andy Grove says that when a company is at the point of no return, it reaches what he calls a "Strategic Inflection Point." Fundamental change is needed. Survival is on the line. Hopefully your company never reaches that point, but if it does, this is as good a story as any to tell. Try this: "Folks, the situation is not getting any better. We are getting clobbered and the time has come to do something. Intel's Andy Grove tells of a meeting he had with Gordon Moore when their company faced an even tougher challenge . . ."

Source

Andrew S. Grove, *Only the Paranoid Survive* (New York: Currency Double-day, 1999), pp. 85–89.

Andy Grove

INTEL

Letting Go

> Customer Reaction to Change
> Challenging Company Dogmas
> Exiting a Business
> Emotional Stake in Decisions

Breaking up is hard to do. Andy Grove knew the decision to exit the memory chip business would be extraordinarily tough for Intel. He tells of the time when the decision wasn't yet ready to be made public but had already been made. He recounts the story of visiting a remote Intel location for dinner with a group of local managers. Debate about the memory business was already long in the air, and sure enough, the issue came up. When asked about what he planned to do to remedy the situation, Grove says he gave an "ambivalent to negative" answer. One person immediately pounced: "Does that mean you can conceive of Intel without being in the memory business?" Grove paused, swallowed hard, and uttered a single word—"Yes." As he then describes it, "All hell broke loose."

The reason for the reaction? What he describes as virtual religious dogmas at Intel. The first was that memories were the company's technology drivers. The other was the need for a full product line to survive. The dinner discussion then went in circles, with Grove ultimately thinking that perhaps smaller steps were needed to exit the business instead of an abrupt break. But delay would only make matters worse. Finally, the decision was made. Pull the Band-Aid off quickly so the pain would be as brief as possible. Then came the tough part: informing customers that Intel was exiting the memory business. To Grove's amazement, however, the unexpected happened. In many cases, customer reaction was—as he puts it—"a big yawn." Most customers had already anticipated the change. Some even said, "It sure took you a long time." Although not clear beforehand, the lesson for Grove was simple: "People who have no emotional stake in a decision can see what needs to be done sooner."

Using This Anecdote

It happens every time. The outside world often sees your business predicament with far greater objectivity than you do. People on the inside are usually naturally resistant to change—even inevitable change—strengthening inertia but delaying the inevitable. Try this: "I know this change seems like the end of the world to us, but I'd like to remind everyone that that's not how the rest of the world sees it. Intel's Andy Grove tells the story of . . ."

Source
Andrew S. Grove, *Only the Paranoid Survive* (New York: Currency Doubleday, 1999), pp. 90–92.

Andy Grove

INTEL

Cassandra Was Right

> Early Warnings
> Listening to Advice
> Middle-Management Sales Force
> Separating Trends from Noise

The blips on the radar screen are telling you something. Grove's "Strategic Inflection Points"—intersections at which a company must make a dramatic change in order to survive—can only be reached when all the evidence is in. But if companies refuse to see the reality around them, not only will they not know they're in trouble, they won't have the internal debate they need to face—and act on—the change needed. Grove says it is critical that senior management listen to the Cassandras in their ranks. (Cassandra was the priestess in Greek mythology who foresaw the fall of Troy. No one believed her at the time. But her warnings proved true.)

In the case of business, the Cassandras you need to heed will most likely come from the ranks of middle management, usually in your sales organization. Why? Because they're often the ones first hit by the winds of change from the *real* world. There's another reason they're a good trip wire: Bad news affects them personally—if they don't make the sale because of inferior products, for example, they don't get their commission. You can bet they'll take that seriously, and if you're not already seeking their advice, they will eventually seek you out with the bad news. Grove tells the story of receiving an email from one such Intel manager in the Asia-Pacific region who was passing along news to Grove that could affect their market position. Grove then asked, whose position was right? Grove's, with an overall view of the business? Or the manager's, who was closer to the competition? "I have learned to respect changes in the tone of messages from people in the field," he says. In this particular story, for example, he decided to follow the news his field manager sent him more carefully than he would have otherwise and eventually initiated a study to look into the matter further.

Using This Anecdote

Business can't be all accelerator and no brakes. You need both. In fact, you need to pay more careful attention to those much closer to the front line of the business than to those intent on delivering nothing but good news. Try this: "As senior leaders in this company, if we are not paying attention to those on the front lines, we are going to fall further behind. Yes, I'm an optimist and I'm bullish about our prospects, but I'm also a realist who can take bad news. Andy Grove tells of how . . ." Or, for inspiring those in middle management: "You're on the front lines in this company. You should be giving the news—the good, the bad, and the ugly—to those above you. If they don't hear it from you, they'll likely never hear it at all."

Source
Andrew S. Grove, *Only the Paranoid Survive* (New York: Currency Double-day, 1999), pp. 108–111.

Andy Grove

INTEL

Make Up Your Mind

> Decisiveness vs. Indecision
> Leadership
> Marketing and Sales Force
> Media

Markets hate indecision. So, too, do employees. A clear directive—whichever way—is often preferable to managing by a never-ending series of fits and starts. Andy Grove tells a story of collaborating with another company and working with a high-ranking executive. On the one hand, this person seemed sold on collaboration. On the other, Grove says he seemed almost "paralyzed" when it came to committing to what was needed to make the collaboration a success.

As Grove recounts, a few days after he met with the CEO of the company that was supposed to be collaborating, that CEO was quoted in the press saying he supported the direction his company and Intel were taking. Bolstered by this good news, Grove tore the article out of the newspaper and waved it in front of his Intel associates saying that, yes, they were in business now! But the following day, the newspaper printed a retraction. The story was *wrong*. It was all a big misunderstanding, and the two companies ended up not working together. Putting aside his own disappointment, Grove saw a lesson in the story. Leaders should *lead* and commit to a direction, not change direction on a daily basis—especially in the media! "Think for a moment what it must feel like to be a marketing or sales manager being buffeted by such ambiguities coming from your boss," he says. "How can you motivate yourself to continue to follow a leader when he appears to be going around in circles?"

Using This Anecdote

Decisiveness is a trait your employees are watching for. There's nothing worse from an employee's perspective than a boss who can't make up his or her mind. Better a decision you may not necessarily 100 percent agree with than no clarity about any direction at all. Try this: "I don't believe in management by media. We need to be decisive, and when we make a decision we need to stick by them and all be on board. Andy Grove tells the story of when . . ."

Source
Andrew S. Grove, *Only the Paranoid Survive* (New York: Currency Doubleday, 1999), pp. 142–143.

Lee Iacocca

CHRYSLER CORPORATION

How Do You Get to Carnegie Hall?

> Appearing in Public
> Practice
> PR Stunts

Practice may not always make perfect, but winging it's way too risky. Chrysler's former chairman Lee Iacocca tells a story from his early years in the automotive industry when he was the assistant sales manager for Ford in the Philadelphia area. That year—1956—Ford decided to promote car safety over speed or performance. The company was particularly proud of its safety padding for the dashboard that would protect passengers in an accident. Ford even sent a film (remember, this was the age before videocassettes, the Internet, and DVDs) to dealers claiming that if you dropped an egg off the side of a two-story building, it would safely bounce undamaged off the fabric.

Ever the consummate marketer, Iacocca loved the idea. He decided to show it to his sales force so they could then cascade the message down the ranks to their customers. But instead of just relying on the film, Iacocca—something of a showman himself—wanted to make his point with more dramatic flair. He would demonstrate it himself. At the meeting of more than one thousand salespeople, he placed some of the fabric strips on the floor and then climbed atop a ladder with a carton of eggs. Bombs away! The first egg missed the fabric altogether smashing on the floor. Splat! The audience roared with laughter. The second egg bounced off the shoulder of the person holding the ladder and again onto the floor—splat! The third and fourth eggs landed on target, but unfortunately broke on impact. The fifth one also landed on the fabric, yet remained intact. This final success earned Iacocca an ironic standing ovation. He writes that he "had plenty of egg on my face" that day and learned two things. First, he jokes that he would never again use eggs at a sales meeting—period. Fair enough. Second: Never, ever come unprepared to a public event, without rehearsing. Whether it's the speech you're about to deliver or the clever PR stunt you're about to do, you reduce the risk of failing in public by practice, practice, practice.

Using This Anecdote

This humorous story can be used to preface an actual stunt (especially one that you've actually practiced!) or to remind people that if they're going to represent the company in public, they had better make sure their presentation is polished and ready. Try this: "I hope this works, I'm reminded of a story I remember from Lee Iacocca's autobiography where a stunt like this went awry . . ." Or "When you go out there and talk with the public, you should be 100 percent certain every-thing is buttoned up and ready to go. I'm reminded of a story from Lee Iacocca early in his career . . ."

Source
Lee Iacocca, *Iacocca: An Autobiography* (New York: Bantam Books, 1984), pp. 38–39.

Lee Iacocca

CHRYSLER CORPORATION

I Demand a Recount!

> Getting Your Numbers Straight
> Learning About the Real World
> Unfairness

Life's not always fair. Lee Iacocca should know—he's got more than his share of stories about life's unfairness, including his firing at Ford before taking the helm at Chrysler. He says that he learned early on how unfair things can be and how the world really works all too often. He tells the story of when he was in the sixth grade and how much he wanted to be captain of the school patrol. He coveted the position because it held a special status—like quarterback of the football team—and it even included its own uniform. He ran enthusiastically for the office, but lost to another boy in a close race, 22–20.

Disappointed by the results, young Iacocca went to the movies with friends that weekend. A classmate in front of him turned around and chided him for losing the election, calling him dumb. Iacocca asked why. The boy then explained that forty-two kids voted in the election—but there were only thirty-eight people in the whole class! *"Can't you count?"* It turned out Iacocca's opponent had stuffed the ballot box. The election was rigged in his opponent's favor! The next school day, an angry Iacocca went to the teacher to say that the election was a fraud. The teacher, however, wasn't moved. She didn't want to make waves and risk a scandal, so she let the results stand. "The incident had a profound effect on me," says Iacocca. "It was my first dramatic lesson that life wasn't always going to be fair."

Using This Anecdote

Luck does not always fall your—or your company's—way. Life can indeed sometimes be unfair. Sometimes we just need to suck it up and move on despite bitter feelings. Try this: "I know how disappointed we all are this deal didn't come through. It was indeed unfair. But this is a recurring theme in business, as it is in life. I'm reminded of a story Lee Iacocca, a man with more than his share of stories about unfairness, had to tell about early in his life . . ." You can also use this anecdote to remind people—humorously—to watch their numbers carefully: "Make sure you count correctly!"

Source
Lee Iacocca, *Iacocca: An Autobiography* (New York: Bantam Books, 1984), p. 15.

> Customer Psychology
> Customer Relations
> Sales/After Sales

Lee Iacocca tells the story of a master salesman he knew early in his career. His name was Murray Kester, a sales manager in Wilkes-Barre, Pennsylvania. Kester—who happened to be related to a renowned comedian of that era, Henny Youngman—was a real pro at motivating and training his sales force, as well as motivating customers. One of the tricks he would use, for example, was to call every customer who bought a car from him about a month or so after the sale. But—in a twist—instead of asking what the customer thought of the car, he would ask what the customers' *friends* thought of the automobile. His reasoning was simple. If you called the customer to ask what he or she thought about the car, the customer might get suspicious, might even think something was wrong with the car. But if you instead asked what the person's friends thought of the new purchase, the customer would most likely tell you how wonderful they thought the car was.

Why? Because even if the person's friends were lukewarm, or outright didn't like the car, it was still too soon for the customer to admit to anyone else that he or she had potentially made an error. The customer still needed to justify in his or her own mind that the purchase was the right one—at least for now. The first hurdle cleared, Kester would then ask if the customer would mind providing the names and numbers of friends who really liked the car since they, too, might be in the market to buy one. "Remember this," writes Iacocca. "Anyone who buys anything—a house, a car, or stocks and bonds—will rationalize his purchase for a few weeks, even if he made a mistake."

Using This Anecdote

It's practically human nature. If a person is ever going to have buyer's remorse, it will set in later, not earlier. Right after making a purchase of any kind, consumers usually stick to their guns and insist the decision was the right one. This is exactly the time to cement the relationship. Try this: "The sales process is not over just because the customer has left the store or the lot. After-sale efforts are important for cementing customer loyalty, too. It reminds me of a story Lee Iacocca mentions from early in his career as an auto executive . . ."

Source
Lee Iacocca, *Iacocca: An Autobiography* (New York: Bantam Books, 1984), pp. 33–34.

Lee Iacocca

CHRYSLER CORPORATION

No "I" in Team

> Ability to Advance
> Ability to Get Along with Others
> Collaboration
> Team Spirit

It's not every day you get advice from a legend. Lee Iacocca tells the story of a private dinner he had with legendary football coach Vince Lombardi, who was a personal friend. During the dinner, Iacocca asked Lombardi what exactly his formula was for putting together a winning team. Lombardi—one of the most successful coaches in football history, for whom the NFL named the Super Bowl trophy in his honor—should know. He had put together more than his share of winning teams during a storybook career. He told Iacocca that the teams all had three things in common. He said first you have to teach all the players the fundamentals of the game and how each of them should play his individual position. Then you have to teach them discipline and how to play as a team. Successful teams have no room for outsized egos or prima donnas.

Still, Lombardi continued, a lot of teams have both those things but don't go on to consistently win games. It was the *third* ingredient that made the difference: how everyone feels about the other members of the team. They have to care for one another. Each player has to be thinking of the welfare of the other guys. He has to think that he needs to do his job well so others can do the same. Call it "team spirit," "esprit de corps," or whatever you want, it works. Iacocca says it's the same in business: Those who work well with others and help them do their jobs well advance in the company. Those who don't usually don't get as far. "There's one thing I hate to see on any executive's evaluation, no matter how talented he may be, and that's the line: 'He has trouble getting along with other people.' To me, it's the kiss of death."

Using This Anecdote

It's corny—but true. There really is no "I" in team. For management teams to work successfully, each team member must not only know his or her job and approach it with discipline, the team player must also be concerned about helping the performance of his or her fellow managers—"No one's perfect, but a team can be." Try this: "We need to work together more as a team, less as a collection of talented individuals. I'm reminded of a story one of the greatest managers in the automotive industry told of discussing team spirit with one of the greatest football coaches in history . . ."

Source
Lee Iacocca, *Iacocca: An Autobiography* (New York: Bantam Books, 1984), pp. 56–57.

Lee Iacocca

CHRYSLER CORPORATION

"I'm a Card-Carrying . . ."

> Government Support
> Political Parties
> Switching Allegiances

Party loyalties can change. Lee Iacocca says he believes the loan guarantees Chrysler received from the U.S. federal government in 1979 would not have been possible under a GOP administration. He reminisces in his autobiography that when he was younger and poorer, during the Depression, his family was Democratic. He says they saw the Democrats as being more on the side of people like them when times were tough. But when times were good—both before and after the Depression—they were Republicans, saying the GOP would do more to help them keep the money they had worked hard to earn rather than pay it to the government in taxes.

Iacocca adds that he went through a similar transformation when he was an adult. When he was at Ford and things were going well, he was a rock-ribbed Republican. But when he took over the helm of Chrysler, which had been failing badly, he writes that the Democrats showed more concern for the thousands of workers about to lose their jobs and took a pragmatic approach to providing loan guarantees to keep the company afloat so he could turn it around. More often than not, interests reflect the way people cast their ballots.

Using This Anecdote

Business needs to work with political parties of all stripes based on interest. Try this: "Politics is a touchy subject, but remember we have to work with political figures of all stripes based on whether they have our best interest in mind. I know you may have some deeply felt political beliefs—and that's fine. But in this case, we have to keep the interests of the company first and foremost. I'm reminded of a story Chrysler's Lee Iaccoca tells . . ."

Source

Lee Iacocca, *Iacocca: An Autobiography* (New York: Bantam Books, 1984), pp. 9–10.

Lee Iacocca

CHRYSLER CORPORATION

Building a Better Mousetrap

> Breaking the Mold
> Design
> Game Changer
> Nothing Succeeds Like Success

Before he became chairman of Chrysler in 1978, Lee Iacocca made his reputation at Ford, where his biggest hit—by far—was the Ford Mustang of the 1960s. His stellar success proved the adage that nothing succeeds like success, and his timing could not have been better. The car, with its good looks and innovative lines, was made to appeal to several market categories at the same time. It was a masterpiece of design you'd be proud to drive in almost any setting, work or leisure.

Like they say, build a better mousetrap and the world will beat a path to your door. Sure enough, that happened—literally. Iacocca tells the story of the Mustang's launch. On the first day the car went on sale nationwide, showrooms were mobbed. In Chicago, one dealer had to lock his doors because of the crush of people outside waiting to get a look. In Garland, Texas, one dealer had fifteen potential buyers actually bidding on a *single* car in the window. The winner was a man who had spent the night sleeping in his car while his check cleared to ensure that he would get that exact model. In Seattle, a truck driver accidentally smashed into a showroom after being so distracted by the distinctive looks of the new Mustang in the window. After a few weeks, Iacocca writes, it became clear they would have to open a second plant to keep up with the demand. As they say in business, these are good problems to have.

Using This Anecdote

Think big and outside the box. The Mustang was a departure from the usual staid and conventional designs coming out of Detroit at the time. Iacocca thought big, took a gamble, and won. The public reaction was proof that this type of thinking can pay huge dividends. Try this: "Folks, the marketplace will ultimately decide whether we're successful or not. But we've got to be different in order to stand out. We've got to capture the attention of consumers who are already bombarded with sameness and have shorter and shorter attention spans. I'm reminded of the success Lee Iacocca had, for example, when he first launched the Ford Mustang, which broke all records . . ."

Source

Lee Iacocca, *Iacocca: An Autobiography* (New York: Bantam Books, 1984), pp. 72–73.

> Firing
> Friends
> Personal Vendetta
> Pettiness

Talk about a difficult boss. Lee Iacocca's story of being fired by Henry Ford II at the Ford Motor Company has all the palace intrigue of a novel. Henry, the grandson and namesake of the company's founder, was determined not only to get rid of Iacocca for personal reasons—albeit not terribly rational ones, given Iacocca's stunning success at Ford—but also to purge everyone who had ever been perceived to be on Iacocca's side! Iacocca tells the story of when the head of Ford public relations received a call from Henry Ford II in the middle of the night. Apparently waking the executive, Ford outright asked him whether he liked Iacocca. When the PR exec answered honestly, yes, he did like Iacocca, Ford told him he was fired and abruptly hung up the phone. Although the order was later rescinded, it was nonetheless a sign of the deep personal enmity Ford felt toward Iacocca.

It didn't stop there. Other colleagues completely disappeared from

Iacocca's life. Almost four years after his firing, the chief stewardess of Ford's air fleet was demoted because she still stayed in touch with Iacocca's wife. Former friends from Ford didn't even show up to his wife's funeral. While Iacocca knew that many Ford employees probably could not reach out to him after he was fired—or risk being fired themselves—he could not understand the behavior of the board members. In his opinion, they should have been a stronger check and balance against this kind of petty, vindictive behavior. They weren't. When Ford told them they had to declare their loyalty to him or Iacocca, the results were clear: Iacocca lost. As a columnist later wrote, calling Henry Ford II a "sixty-year-old adolescent": "If a guy like Iacocca's job isn't safe, is yours?" Writing in his autobiography, Iacocca says: "My father always used to say that when you die, if you've got five real friends, you've had a great life. I found out in a hurry."

Using This Anecdote

Friendships can be elusive in business anyway, but when a dysfunctional management stands in the way, don't expect much. This anecdote can be used to demonstrate how *not* to treat people in the workplace—even if those individuals are eventually let go by the company for whatever reason, legitimate or not. Try this: "The last thing we want here is a poisonous environment where people are constantly taking sides and looking over their shoulders. I'm reminded of what happened to Lee Iacocca when he was fired at Ford . . ."

Source
Lee Iacocca, *Iacocca: An Autobiography* (New York: Bantam Books, 1984), pp. 130–132.

Lee Iacocca

CHRYSLER CORPORATION

Madison Avenue Miracle

> Ability to Move on a Dime
> Advertising
> Creativity
> Speed

Lee Iacocca wanted more from Madison Avenue. He tells the story of how he was unimpressed with the marketing department when he became CEO at Chrysler. A marketing-driven executive himself, he recounts how he decided to replace the two ad agencies then working for Chrysler—Young & Rubicam and BBDO—with Kenyon & Eckhardt (K&E). Iacocca announced the $150 million move, which had been kept a closely guarded secret, at a March 1979 press conference in New York City, in what was one of the biggest corporate account changes in advertising of that era. His choice of K&E had been based on the creative work the agency had done while he was at Ford. To sweeten the deal, he offered K&E a five-year contract—something largely unheard of in the advertising business—as well as the opportunity to become more deeply embedded within the company.

He reasoned that if the new agency were more deeply involved with the process of creating the car—instead of being brought in at the last minute as is usually the case—they would be more creative. The earlier in the process they gave their best advice, the better, especially when it came to naming new cars. For example, one of K&E's first decisions was to bring back the symbol of the ram, which had been used before with Dodge trucks. Agency research showed customers wanted trucks that were rugged and dependable. The ram moniker communicated those attributes, and soon Chrysler was winning over customers who previously wouldn't have considered Dodge. Iacocca also says one of the biggest advantages to the new arrangement was speed. In one example, he says that they decided on a Thursday at 4 p.m. to offer customers a new financing rate. The agency immediately began filming. By 5 a.m. Friday, the commercial was done. By Saturday, the spot was already on the air. By any business's standards, that's incredibly fast.

Using This Anecdote

The quick turnaround Chrysler's ad agency was able to effect was an impressive feat, especially for the late 1970s. Try this: "When it comes to marketing, we need to be able to respond quickly in the digital age. Heck, almost thirty years ago, Lee Iacocca was getting commercials on the air with a less than seventy-two-hour turnaround time—years before digitization made all of this much, much easier. He tells the story of when . . ."

Source
Lee Iacocca, *Iacocca: An Autobiography* (New York: Bantam Books, 1984), pp. 178–181.

Lee Iacocca

CHRYSLER CORPORATION

Equality of Sacrifice

> Leading by Example
> Personal Sacrifice
> Salary

Talk about pressure. Lee Iacocca says the massive effort to save Chrysler from bankruptcy was like waging a war. And he was the four-star general in charge of ensuring that the company stayed afloat and that the jobs of thousands of employees would not be in jeopardy. No small task. With the U.S. Congress having just passed the Loan Guarantee Act in 1979, Iacocca did not stop and rest on his laurels. He tells the story of how he continued to fight on publicly. Iacocca well knew that leadership meant leading not by words alone but by deeds. As a result, so long as Chrysler was still experiencing difficult times, he decided to reduce his own salary to $1 a year—not to be a martyr, but to set an example. He says that only then could he look the union president in the eye and ask him what labor was willing to do to help out in tough times. "I wanted our employees and our suppliers to be thinking: 'I can follow this guy who sets that kind of example,'" he says.

He calls it "equality of sacrifice." "If everybody is suffering equally, you can move a mountain," he writes. The trick is to make sure no one shirks his or her responsibility or appears to be freeloading. Otherwise, the whole thing comes tumbling down. He likens it to a family being given a loan from a rich uncle and then proving they can pay him back. Soon, others were starting to notice Iacocca's sincerity and offering to pitch in. Entertainment legends of that era, including Frank Sinatra, Bob Hope, and Pearl Bailey, all offered to help. Sinatra shot commercials for Chrysler, and Bill Cosby performed in front of twenty thousand employees. Others pitched in as well. Not one asked for a dime. In the end, Iacocca says it wasn't the government loans that ultimately saved Chrysler, but hundreds of individual acts of sacrifice—large and small—that made it possible. But he had to lead by example to get the ball rolling and convince people that he and his cause were sincere.

Using This Anecdote

Hopefully, times aren't as tough at your company as they were when Lee Iacocca led a struggling Chrysler through its darkest days. His sincere story of sacrifice and setting an example for the rest of the company is a good one to use especially if your company's leadership is contemplating a similar move. Try this: "Look, times are tough. We all have to make sacrifices, but I cannot ask you to do so if I myself don't do my share. I'm reminded of a story Lee Iacocca told in his autobiography about what he did during the depths of the bankruptcy crisis his company faced . . ."

Source

Lee Iacocca, *Iacocca: An Autobiography* (New York: Bantam Books, 1984), pp. 229–231.

> American Values
> Immigrants
> Hard Work
> Worries About the Future

Former Chrysler chairman Lee Iacocca writes in his autobiography how he had been asked by then president Ronald Reagan to serve as chairman of the Statue of Liberty–Ellis Island Centennial Commission while still trying to save Chrysler from bankruptcy. Even though he had more than enough to do back in Detroit, Iacocca gladly accepted the position as a labor of love to honor his immigrant parents who had come to the United States from Italy. "My parents were greenhorns," he says. "They didn't know the language. They didn't know what to do when they came here. They were poor and they had nothing. [Ellis Island] was a part of my being—not the place itself, but what it stood for and how tough an experience it was."

Iacocca writes that many Americans are the descendants of immigrants to this country and owe much to the sacrifice their forebears made during often much tougher times. He recounts how—during the Depression—his mother didn't complain about having to work in the silk mills so her son could have lunch money for school. He says that while the Statute of Liberty may be the ultimate symbol of freedom, Ellis Island is the true reality of America's immigrant experience. Freedom is a gift, but it's just the beginning. To survive and make a better life for the next generation, you have to pay a price through hard work. People should not worry too much about the future so long as the example of the sacrifices made by their immigrant forebears are kept alive and honored. "What the last fifty years taught us was the difference between right and wrong, that only hard work succeeds, that there are no free lunches. You have to be productive. Those are the values that made this country great."

Using This Anecdote

Sometimes you have to remind people of the values that made this country unique and why it continues to be a magnet for immigrants from all over the world. What are they? Hard work, not "hardly working." "Can-do optimism" not "Can't-do defeatism." Yes, sometimes people *do* need to be reminded. Try this: "This is truly a great country, but sometimes amid all our prosperity and comfort, we forget *how* we got here. It wasn't preordained. It was *earned*. I'm reminded of how Lee Iacocca described it in his autobiography . . ."

Source
Lee Iacocca, *Iacocca: An Autobiography* (New York: Bantam Books, 1984), pp. 339–341.

> Management Style
> Putting One's Stamp on Something
> Taking Credit

Long known for his unorthodox management style, Apple founder Steve Jobs was legendary for his hands-on technique. For example, according to one programmer, he would come into an employee's cubicle, sit down, and start toying with whatever the person happened to be working on. Although Jobs wasn't always entirely knowledgeable about the technical side of what was being developed, he would start making suggestions on how to improve the project. He'd then disappear, often not to be seen again until much later.

Employees soon caught on. They realized the circuitous game they apparently had to play in order to get Jobs to sign on to a new idea. If their idea was something Jobs hadn't thought of before, the tactic was to propose it to him—with the full knowledge ahead of time that he would more than likely reject it outright at first. Then, the waiting game would begin. Sure enough, Jobs would often be back telling everyone later about the great idea he had which was—more or less—the same idea he had previously rejected. Whatever works. Some even joked that Jobs had his own "reality distortion field," but they forgave this tactic of nonrecognition. More often than not, he just needed to mull over an idea in his head until it developed to the point where he was satisfied it was *his* idea. Only then was he ready to present it to others. Though others quickly realized the game, no one was entirely sure whether Jobs himself was being calculating about it or whether it was unintended on his part. Either way, the end products that stemmed from those ideas—however they were developed—always spoke for themselves.

Using This Anecdote

Let the customer take credit for a good idea. Some people just need to make an idea their own before they can truly *believe*. In this case, Jobs's employees quickly learned the game and apparently ended up playing it well to their advantage, anticipating ahead of time how Jobs would act rather than getting angry at him. Try this: "There's more than one way to get what you want, and sometimes the most direct route is not the best way. We all know psychology plays a big role in business. There's the story about Steve Jobs . . ."

Source

Jeffrey Young, *Icon—Steve Jobs: The Second Greatest Act in the History of Business* (New York: John Wiley & Sons Inc., 2005), pp. 75–76.

Steve Jobs

APPLE

Connecting the Dots

> Destiny
> Following Your Passion
> Overcoming Obstacles
> Trusting Your Gut

He wasn't exactly born with a silver spoon in his mouth. With all the wealth and fame Steve Jobs currently enjoys, it's hard to imagine the adversity Jobs had to overcome to get where he is today. Put up for adoption by his unwed mother, he was taken in by a working-class couple who had limited means to send him to college. Although he eventually went to Reed College in California, he didn't graduate. Throughout his limited college experience, he needed to sleep on friends' floors because he couldn't afford a dorm room. To get by, he returned Coke bottles for the deposit money. He says the one good meal of the week he enjoyed was every Sunday at a Hare Krishna temple he had to walk seven miles to reach.

After dropping out of college, Jobs decided to continue taking classes, but he didn't feel compelled to take any of the required courses—he decided to take only those that interested him. One such course was calligraphy—a major strength at Reed. There he learned the ins and outs of typography, a skill that would later help him when designing the Macintosh, which stood out from other computers for the beauty and variety of its fonts—a feature that has since been widely imitated. The key, though, is the fact that had he not dropped out, he probably wouldn't have been able to follow his instincts and take that course that eventually helped his fledgling product stand out in the marketplace. "You can't connect the dots looking forward, you can only connect them looking backwards," Jobs says. "So you have to trust that the dots will somehow connect in your future. You have to trust in something—your gut, life, karma, whatever. This approach has never let me down."

Using This Anecdote

Many business leaders have risen from hardscrabble circumstances. Steve Jobs is no exception. One of the keys for him was trusting his instincts and following what captivated him and became his passion. The same may be said for people in other businesses. Unless they're working in areas where they have a passion for what they do—whether it's sales, accounting, marketing, R&D, supply chain management, whatever—they're not likely to be at peak performance. Try this: "Sometimes you have to follow your gut when it comes to putting the right people in the right jobs. There's no magic formula. I'm reminded of a story Steve Jobs told . . ."

Source
Steve Jobs, commencement address, Stanford University, June 12, 2005: http://news.stanford.edu/news/2005/june15/jobs-061505.html.

Steve Jobs

APPLE

"You're Fired"

> Getting Fired
> Following Your Passion
> Second Acts
> Starting Over

It was perhaps one of the most public firings in recent American business history. In 1985, at age thirty, the man who had founded Apple, the person behind the Macintosh computer, Steve Jobs, was himself out of a job. The Apple board of directors decided his vision no longer fit with the company. *Boom!* Genius entrepreneur one day—unemployed working stiff the next. Jobs tells the story of how he saw himself as a public failure. He apologized to the previous generation of entrepreneurs, including David Packard and Bob Noyce. For months, he didn't know what to do. Then he realized something important. He may have been rejected at one company, but he didn't fall out of love with what he liked to do best.

In hindsight, Jobs would later say that his being fired from the same company he founded turned out to be the *best* thing that ever happened to him. Why? Because "the heaviness of success was replaced by the lightness of being a beginner again . . . it freed me to enter one of the most creative periods of my life." During the next five years, he went on to Pixar, a movie studio that would later produce such hits as *Toy Story* and *Monsters, Inc.*, and eventually made his way back to Apple through NeXT, a company that built computer workstations. His return to Apple would end up being one of American business's most famous—and most successful—second acts. "It was awful tasting medicine, but I guess the patient needed it," Jobs once said in a commencement speech. "The only way to do great work is to love what you do. If you haven't found it yet, keep looking. Don't settle."

Using This Anecdote

There's no way to sugarcoat losing one's job—it's rough, it's unfair, it's no picnic. But sometimes it can be exactly the catalyst for change an individual needs to succeed in the long run. The same can be said for companies overall. Companies also need to follow their passion (that is, focus on what they do best). Sometimes they need to fail at a venture before they realize the right path they should be on. Try this: "Not every venture works out. Neither does every job. The lesson, though, is that companies—like individuals—should always pursue their passion, what they're good at. I'm reminded of Steve Jobs . . ."

Source
Steve Jobs, commencement address, Stanford University, June 12, 2005: http://news.stanford.edu/news/2005/june15/jobs-061505.html.

Steve Jobs

APPLE

Stay Hungry, Stay Foolish

> Facing Death
> Following Your Heart
> Living Your Own Life

Your time here is limited; make the most of it. Steve Jobs says looking at the rest of your life while always keeping an eye on the finish line is perhaps the best way to lead a rich and fulfilling life. Jobs tells the story of a close brush with death at age forty-eight. In October 2003, following a routine scan, he was diagnosed with pancreatic cancer—a normally incurable form of the disease. Doctors broke the news to him that he had three to six months to live. He was advised to go home, put his affairs in order, and prepare for the inevitable. Later that evening, they used a scope, which they placed down his digestive tract and through his stomach and intestines, to get a few cells from the pancreas. Jobs was sedated throughout the whole procedure, and his wife later told him how she watched as the doctors looked at the sample cells under the microscope and began to weep—*from joy*. It turned out Jobs actually had a rare form of pancreatic cancer that was indeed curable. Surgery followed and proved successful.

That brush with death had a profound effect on Jobs. "Your time is limited, so don't waste it living someone else's life. Don't be trapped by dogma . . . Don't let the noise of others' opinions drown out your own inner voice. And most important, have the courage to follow your heart and intuition. They already know what you want to become. Everything else is secondary."

Using This Anecdote

Following your inner voice is a common theme with leaders in many fields. It's definitely career advice worth heeding. Sometimes it takes a brush with death for people to realize exactly what that inner voice is saying—*follow it*. Try this: "Some of the best advice often comes from bitter experience. Steve Jobs tells the story of the time he was diagnosed with cancer and how that only reinforced his views on life . . ."

Source
Steve Jobs, commencement address, Stanford University, June 12, 2005: http://news.stanford.edu/news/2005/june15/jobs-061505.html.

Steve Jobs

APPLE

It Can't Be Done!

> Design Innovation
> Comfort Zone
> Stretch Goals

Apple's innovative designs have won many awards, not to mention the hearts of some of the most devoted electronics consumers out there. But not every design the company came up with was the result of collaborative, warm and fuzzy efforts. In fact, some of them were the result of the company being given a challenge seen as impossible at the time and then expending the effort to meet the goal to make the boss happy. There's a story about what happened during the development of the Macintosh in the early 1980s. Steve Jobs walked into a design meeting and tossed a telephone book on the table with a loud thud. "That's how big the Macintosh can be. Nothing bigger will make it. Consumers won't stand for it any larger," he's quoted as saying. He added that he wanted to see something that was taller, not wider. He then spun on his heels and walked out, leaving the disbelieving employees in his wake. It couldn't be done, some said. No way. The electronics to run it couldn't fit into anything *that* size.

Everyone around the table also knew Jobs wasn't the type of person to take no for an answer. As inflexible and frustrating as direct orders like that can be, they can also inspire people to try harder than ever before—motivating them to rise to the occasion. Sure enough, the technical difficulties were overcome, and the familiar, iconic, vertical-style machines changed little after being introduced. Goals are great; stretch goals are even better. What's often needed is a firm nudge to get people to leave their comfort zones far behind.

Using This Anecdote

Sometimes it's better to be handed an assignment that seems impossible at first. Then rise to the occasion rather than settling for standing in place. A concrete—but difficult—goal is better than no goal at all. Try this: "Companies don't get ahead by standing in place. They get ahead by pushing the envelope further and further each time. Sometimes it takes a strong demand from the top to get people to get out of their comfort zone and really start innovating . . ."

Source
Jeffrey Young, *Icon—Steve Jobs: The Second Greatest Act in the History of Business* (New York: John Wiley & Sons Inc., 2005), pp. 76–77.

Steve Jobs

APPLE

"Pay No Attention to That Man Behind the Curtain"

> Practice
> Preparation
> Presenting
> Technical Glitches

Showmanship is part of the job. Steve Jobs, one of the most successful contemporary businesspersons, is also quite possibly one of the business world's most gifted public presenters. Known for keeping his audience's rapt attention, he's a "natural." For product launches, for example, his staff might schedule rehearsals and he may be handed a speech, but he's likely not to show up or read the speech. He's more likely to spend time with the technical crew, showing them how he wants to present the product, what lighting cues he's going use, and how the show should look and feel so the timing is just right. Call it "software meets stagecraft" or "Hollywood meets Silicon Valley"— call it whatever you want—it works for him. And his audiences are usually hanging on his every word.

But . . . as we all know, even the best-laid plans can sometimes go awry—even for a person of Jobs's stature. One time, when Jobs was onstage introducing Apple's first Laser Writer, at the dramatic point in the presentation when he was going to show how the printer worked, he hit the Send button, and voilà—*nothing happened.* Silence. No printing. Without missing a beat, Jobs kept right on talking, keeping his audience's attention the whole time as a team of white-jacketed technicians suddenly appeared from backstage. They began feverishly working on the problem until it was fixed, then vanished into the darkness offstage. Jobs—who in the meantime had continued talking as if nothing had happened—went back to exactly where he had left off and the show went on. Impressive. Not many people could pull that off with such aplomb.

Using This Anecdote

If you are making a presentation, it always pays to be *really* prepared. Practice, practice, practice. But be ready for the inevitable glitches that can and do occur despite even the best preparation. Use them in a humorous way so you get your audience on your side. Try this: "Now, I'll be the first to admit I'm not the most technologically gifted individual here, and let's hope it doesn't happen now, but I take heart in the fact that it can happen to the best of them. Even Steve Jobs has encountered technical difficulties, like the time . . ."

Source
Jeffrey Young, *Icon—Steve Jobs: The Second Greatest Act in the History of Business* (New York: John Wiley & Sons Inc., 2005), pp. 272–273.

> Creativity
> Naming a Product
> Rejecting a Winning Idea

Have you ever heard of an electronic device called the "Dulcimer"? Probably not. Unless you happened to be working at Apple a while back—and even then, you might not have known this was the code name for the product that would eventually become one of their most iconic devices to date: the iPod. A product's name can often make or break success—at least as far as marketing is concerned. But the naming process is not always simple. Part of the task was easier in this particular case, however, because Jobs had already settled on the tagline of "1,000 songs in your pocket." The bottom line: The future product name didn't have to refer to music after all. In discussing the options, Jobs repeatedly referred to the company's strategy of being a hub—of connecting things. During the discussion, one person said that the ultimate example of a hub would be a spaceship. Just like that scene in the classic Stanley Kubrick movie *2001: A Space Odyssey*, you might leave the ship in a smaller craft—a pod—only to return eventually to the mother ship.

Several names were then written down on index cards. Jobs went through them—one by one—creating two piles. One was for maybes, another for no's. When the "iPod" card came up, guess where it ended up? *Nope.* It was placed with the rejects. Jobs then asked for others' opinions. One person went back to the reject pile and pulled out the "iPod" card. As the employee described it, this name made the most sense given the hub analogy. Plus, it was easy to remember. After the meeting, Jobs began testing "iPod" and several other names both inside and outside the company. He later said he was sold on the iPod name. One of its benefits—aside from being memorable and sleek—is that the name doesn't describe the device, so it can remain unchanged even as the technology evolves. The ultimate irony was that it turned out Apple had already trademarked the name "iPod" for an Internet kiosk product they had considered but dropped. Many were unaware that they had already owned the name in the first place! Even if the company's right hand didn't always know what the left hand was doing, creativity kept them moving forward.

Using This Anecdote

This is a good anecdote to use when talking about the importance of creativity, particularly in tasks like naming a product. Keep your main metaphor in mind—such as the hub in this case—and work from there. It can also be used to show that sometimes good fortune can visit a company even if the corporate right hand doesn't always know what the corporate left hand is doing! Try this: "I know how hard it is to name our new X . . . You may not believe this, but the name iPod was rejected by none other than Steve Jobs when it was first considered, too . . ."

Source
Leander Kahney, *Inside Steve's Brain* (New York: Portfolio, 2009), p. 227.

> Global Business
> Diversity
> Multicultural Talent

We live in a truly global economy today with markets more open than ever. So, too, is the market for talent. Alcoa's chairman and CEO Klaus Kleinfeld is no stranger to contemporary business being global and multicultural. After leading Siemens AG, Germany's electronics and electrical engineering giant, the Bremen, Germany, native would go on to head an icon of American business—Alcoa, the world's largest aluminum producer. In an anecdote illustrating the global nature of business today, he tells the story of a trip he took from the United States to Alcoa's plant in Fjarðaál, Iceland.

The company's jet, carrying the most senior leaders, flying in from an Alcoa plant visit in Canada, landed at the airport in Reykjavík at 4 a.m. A bleary-eyed Icelandic passport officer went out to the tarmac and watched as the passengers from this "American" flight started to deplane. The first person off the jet presented his Norwegian passport; the second, an Australian passport; the third, a Canadian passport; the fourth, an

Australian passport; and the fifth, Kleinfeld, a German passport. Finally, the sixth person emerged and presented his American passport. His name? Mohammad Zaidi, the Indian-born head of Alcoa's technology division, who had earlier spent his career in Great Britain and Germany. All of them were members of Alcoa's executive management team. Welcome to today's global economy. As Kleinfeld says, "Talent is today's only real sustainable competitive advantage." When you can find the best and brightest all around the world, you have a leg up. Talent today goes where it's most needed—and it comes from all over.

Using This Anecdote

Managers and executives who want to develop a sustainable advantage in business should look to their *people*. Business today is more global than ever, so in order to succeed, you need to develop high-performance teams from all over the world, and tap into those individuals with varied experiences and perspectives. Try this: "To illustrate just how global even American companies are these days, let me tell you the story Klaus Kleinfeld of Alcoa tells of a flight he took to Iceland. It illustrates his personal mantra, 'Nobody's perfect, but a team can be.'"

Source
Personal interview, New York City, May 11, 2011.

Klaus Kleinfeld

ALCOA

The Dog Ate My Homework

> Consequences of Our Choices
> Setting Goals and Priorities
> Taking Responsibility

Alcoa's German-born chairman and CEO Klaus Kleinfeld hardly seemed predestined to head both the American aluminum giant and—prior to that—Germany's largest electrical engineering company, Siemens AG. His parents were refugees who had fled communist East Germany to freedom in West Germany during the Cold War. His father, an engineer in Bremen, Germany, died of a heart attack when Kleinfeld was only ten years old. An only child, Kleinfeld soon started working as a stock boy in a local supermarket to help support his widowed mother. "It was a rough time, but I've been working practically every day of my life since then and I can't imagine not working."

One day, though, he let work get in the way of completing his homework. Although he was a very good student, he got a bad grade on that particular assignment. After class, Kleinfeld went to see the teacher and explained that his after-school work had prevented him from completing the assignment. The teacher listened and then answered in a polite but firm manner: "Klaus, we all have the same amount of time. You chose to use it differently. You set *your* own priorities. It is my obligation as your teacher to clearly let you know that I disagree with your choice. And you have to learn to live with the consequences of your choices." Kleinfeld says that lesson has stuck with him ever since. There are only twenty-four hours in the day. No matter who you are, it's up to you to use that time well and it's up to you to take responsibility for your actions.

Using This Anecdote

Each of us has the same amount of time in any given day. The question is how we *use* that time. Forget excuses; try responsibility. This anecdote can be used to show how one successful CEO learned his lesson early in life that there are consequences for our decisions and that—whatever the hardships—we still must take responsibility for our actions. Try this: "I know there are often extenuating circumstances, but excuses won't cut it for long. Let me tell you the story of one successful CEO who learned that lesson early on in life . . ."

Source
Personal interview, New York City, May 11, 2011.

Klaus Kleinfeld

ALCOA

Nobody's Perfect, but a Team Can Be

> Creating High-Performance Teams That Get Results
> Using All Skills
> Working Toward a Common Goal

Long before he became Alcoa's CEO, Klaus Kleinfeld worked at Siemens in Germany. He says he was particularly impressed by the caliber of a consulting group he was a member of, and he noticed one interesting phenomenon. Kleinfeld observed that some of the consulting teams were brilliant in their analysis but got no traction when it came to impacting the business. Other teams weren't as sharp in their analysis, but they still managed to successfully change their clients' business in the right direction.

As Kleinfeld recalls: "I realized two things. First, there were two dimensions that needed to be present to generate impact—analytics as well as social skills to get people behind your ideas. Second, rarely do all skills needed for great success reside in one individual. But, if you can align a group of people with different skills around a common understanding and a common purpose, the success will multiply and far outstrip any one of the individual's expectations. They will truly experience that 'nobody's perfect, but a team can be.'" Kleinfeld adds that he's seen what can happen when people experience the benefits of teamwork in action and companies benefit from the results—they quickly become believers. "Once they have experienced this," Kleinfeld says, "it becomes an addiction to create high-performance teams and go the extra mile."

Using This Anecdote

It's not just the shopworn phrase "There's no 'I' in team." There really *are* benefits to working in teams. One person may be brilliant at crunching the numbers but shy when it comes to people skills. Another may be your best ambassador for culture change, but not the best person to handle project management, and so forth. Business today is far too complex for any one individual to have all the skills necessary to do everything perfectly. That's why assembling high-performance teams and aligning them toward a common goal may be your secret weapon for business success. Try this: "Business today doesn't need the Lone Ranger. What we need are people who can do their best working on *teams*. That's the secret to success nowadays. Alcoa's CEO has a great story about this . . ."

Source
Personal interview, New York City, May 11, 2011.

Jacques Nasser

FORD MOTOR COMPANY

If It Ain't Broke, Don't Fix It

> Stopping a Questionable Idea
> Focusing on What Really Counts

Jacques Nasser, former CEO of the Ford Motor Company, knows how important it is for a company to understand its brand identity. He tells the story of some employees in Ford's consumer research department who were determined to change the look of the grille on Ford's Explorer model. Although Nasser was skeptical of the effort, the team went ahead with the experiment anyhow.

One weekend, the Ford team invited about one hundred consumers armed with clipboards to view and compare some fifteen grilles and write down their opinions. They did so, looking carefully at each and recording their impressions. When they had finished, they then discussed their opinions and tabulated their results. The original Ford Explorer grille was the hands-down winner. The only person who wasn't surprised was Jacques Nasser. That grille was part of the company's brand essence, and in Nasser's opinion, there were bigger fish out there to fry—and other expenses more mission-critical to the business—than tests like this one. It was important that his employees understood the company's brand identity and its relation to its consumers. It was also important not to tamper with a winning formula.

Using This Anecdote

Nasser makes an important point: *If it ain't broke, don't fix it*, especially if it's something as important as the company's brand essence. Time is better spent on other pursuits instead of tinkering with what you know already works. This anecdote can be used to head off a bad idea or stop one in its tracks. Try this: "I think we need to focus on much bigger challenges here. This reminds me of a story at Ford Motor Company, where they spent time and effort on changing something only to realize they had the right formula after all . . ."

Source
Harvard Business Review: Interviews with CEOs (Cambridge, MA: Harvard Business School Press, 2000), p. 17.

Indra Nooyi

PEPSICO

We Are Family

> Work-Life Balance
> Kids
> Secrets

Families stick together. Indra Nooyi, PepsiCo's CEO, has said many times that she views her company as one big extended family. Because she came from a middle-class family in southern India, this was hardly a big jump for her. Everyone pitches in, and she says finding the right work-life balance is critical not just for personal reasons, but business as well. If you want to attract the best and brightest, you'll need to accommodate the fact that these individuals also have lives outside the office.

She tells the story of how employees would be allowed to bring their children to the offices at PepsiCo. She says sometimes her then nine-year-old daughter would come home from school and miss being with her mom. She'd then be taken to the office around 5 p.m. and sit with her mom. If Nooyi was too busy, she'd start walking around to the other executives to see if they had time to spare. In one story, she tells of how her daughter dropped in on Don Kendall, a PepsiCo senior executive and cofounder who was eighty-one years old at the time. She asked him if he had time to talk and he said yes. Nooyi's daughter then began pouring out everything her mom was doing and saying at home—to the founder of the company, no less! Nooyi was embarrassed that her daughter was "spilling the beans" about her home life, but this companionable dialogue gave Kendall real insight into Nooyi's daily life—and, of course, gave him the chance to make a new young friend. "At the end of the day," she says, "it is about co-opting the whole ecosystem around you to help you bring up your kids."

Using This Anecdote

Work-life balance is a major issue at most companies. This cute anecdote is a good one for illustrating that even top executives have work-life balance issues and that even those at the top have to be flexible when it comes to finding a balance between office and home. Try this: "In order to attract the type of top talent this company needs, we have to be more mindful of employees' work-life balance issues. I'm reminded of a charming story Indra Nooyi at PepsiCo tells . . ."

Source
Dartmouth College, Tuck School of Business: CEO Speaker Series, September 23, 2002.

Indra Nooyi

PEPSICO

Dress to Be Yourself—Success Will Follow

> Being Oneself
> Core Beliefs
> Immigrants
> Overcoming Odds

Indra Nooyi overcame tremendous odds to become head of PepsiCo. She says she entered corporate America with three strikes against her. First, she was a woman. Second, she was an immigrant. Third, she was a person of color. But despite these odds, she succeeded and then some. She grew up in a middle-class family in Chennai, a city in the southern part of India. As a young person, she was extremely ambitious and driven, eventually earning her way into Yale University's MBA program. Still, when she came to the United States for her studies, she had no safety net. While at Yale, she had virtually no money of her own. Had she failed, it would have been back on the next flight home. She eventually got a job as a receptionist at a Connecticut company, working the midnight to 5 a.m. shift and struggling to put together $50 to buy a Western suit for her first corporate job interview.

Having finally scraped together enough money to buy a suit, she felt uncomfortable in the new and unfamiliar clothes. The interview ultimately didn't result in a job offer. She then turned to her professor for advice. The reply? Be yourself and stick to what makes you comfortable. She then wore her traditional Indian sari dress to the next interview. She got the job. It's impossible to say for sure, but if the clothes probably didn't make or break either interview, the attitude most likely did. Being comfortable with herself likely projected the confidence Nooyi needed. She says she's taken her professor's advice to heart ever since. She's decided to risk being herself and let the chips fall where they may instead of trying to be someone she's not. "I'm so comfortable in myself," she says, "I don't have to be American to play in the corporate life."

Using This Anecdote

Yes, she went to Yale. But not many students—at any university—are willing to work the midnight to 5 a.m. shift just to be able to afford an interview suit. Nooyi's story of overcoming the odds and deciding to be herself is an inspirational one and a success story for women and men alike. Try this: "One of the keys to success in business is to do what you do best, and to have the courage to be yourself. People will know when you're really being you and respect you for it. I'm reminded of a story from PepsiCo's Indra Nooyi . . ."

Source
"Life Stories to Inspire: Indra Nooyi," December 31, 2008: http://hrlink.in/news/life-stories-to-inspire-indra-nooyi-ceo-pepsico.

Indra Nooyi

PEPSICO

Hard Work

> Work Ethic
> Proving Oneself
> Getting an Edge

Competitive genes must run in her family. Indra Nooyi says that she's been so used to working hard and achieving all her life that if she's not working hard, she thinks something is wrong. She tells the story of how her family in India instilled an extremely strong work ethic in her since an early age. She says her grandfather was especially tough on her, saying: "The only thing that matters in life is grades." She recounts the story of how her class was given grades at the end of every month and the students were then ranked based on the results.

She says that on the days report cards were issued, her grandfather would wait at the door to scrutinize results. "If you didn't get one of the first three ranks of the class," she says, "you might as well kill yourself on the way back from school because he was going to kill you." Sometimes her older sister would beat her in the rankings and she'd have to apply herself even more. When she told her grandfather that she wanted to be a rock star or play sports, he'd answer, "Forget it. You are going to study hard." The lesson has stuck ever since. The other lesson she learned from her family was the need to do a job as thoroughly as possible and be better than the next person. "You cannot let anyone down," she says. "If I am given a job, people who work with me . . . will tell you that if Indra is dying she will make sure the job gets done because I just don't know any other way to do the job."

Using This Anecdote

It's been said that you don't have to be absolutely perfect at what you do—but you do have to try harder than the next person. Giving it that extra edge is important in ensuring you're at your personal best and helping your company stay on top. Try this: "Striving for excellence is something that should be celebrated and encouraged. We each have to give it our best shot and then some. Indra Nooyi at Pepsi-Co has known about the pressure to succeed from a very early age . . ."

Source
Dartmouth College, Tuck School of Business: CEO Speaker Series, September 23, 2002.

> Buying into a Vision
> Change
> Communication
> Leadership

Call it *Survivor* for MBAs. Indra Nooyi tells a story of when she was in business school at Yale years ago. One of the exercises they did to gain insights into each student's leadership qualities was to have small groups pretend they were stranded in a desert or in the Arctic. The group would be presented with ten items to aid their "survival." They were allowed to choose only five items, however, so they had to prioritize and cooperate. As the students were working—or *not* working—together, the professors would be watching from behind a one-way mirror, observing group dynamics and taking notes on how they problem-solved as a team.

Nooyi says this exercise was one of the most valuable during her studies. One of the key lessons she says she learned was the challenge of how you bring others along with you—how you get them to buy into your vision. The first step, she says, is to understand all the points of view of those involved and to try and craft a better or new vision. The key? Communication. "It is communication all the time," she says. "I would say you might even argue that it is overcommunication . . ." If you convince your management below you, you've started the act of change. "They carry the message to other people and pretty soon you have this movement take root," she says. Not everyone will come on board, however. She says some 10 percent will resist change and sometimes become the casualties of the new direction. Still, she says that even among those who left the company, many later regretted the decision and some even returned.

Using This Anecdote

Communication is one of the keys to effective leadership. Nooyi's example of being stranded in a desert—or at least pretending to be— is great for reminding people that leaders can't exactly coerce a company into working together. Company members have to be convinced to do so through persuasive communication. Try this: "I know change is not easy, but the key to gaining acceptance is not hoping people will sign on; it's making our case over and over and over again. We cannot communicate enough, frankly. I'm reminded of a story Pepsi-Co's Indra Nooyi tells . . ."

Source
Dartmouth College, Tuck School of Business: CEO Speaker Series, September 23, 2002.

David Packard

HEWLETT-PACKARD

Top Shelf

> Entering the Retail Market
> Sales and Distribution
> Switching Business Models

Call it an early misstep. HP's cofounders David Packard and Bill Hewlett are widely credited with creating what would eventually become California's Silicon Valley—one of the country's greatest economic success stories and still an engine for high-tech growth. Working from a one-car garage turned workshop on Addison Avenue in Palo Alto—later recognized as a California Historical Landmark—the duo helped usher in America's high-tech era.

David Packard tells the story of the company's first foray into the consumer market. They had just started manufacturing a product called the "HP 35" handheld calculator. The calculator's development was tough enough. It now also required new delivery channels. Up until then, the company had essentially made products to order for customers. That model would no longer work in this case. Packard tells the story of one of his engineers, Bill Terry, who paid a sales call on Macy's department store in San Francisco. The store was interested in beefing up its electronics department. Terry showed the manager the product, got his initial interest, and starting talking about customer orders and deliveries. The manager looked Terry squarely in the eye and said: "You young boys don't understand. I don't sell anything unless I have it in the store." *Oops.* As Packard writes, it was their first initiation into the consumer market. They'd have to build to fill shelves from now on. And they'd have to start getting used to a new way of getting their products in the hands of consumers.

Using This Anecdote

Even big companies sometimes have to take baby steps at first. This story can be a good one to remind audiences that companies—and people—often need to climb steep learning curves before they reach their full potential. Try this: "I know we're new at this, but every company, even though they've achieved success, has to face the fact that they don't know everything and need to learn. David Packard of HP tells the story . . ."

Source

David Packard, *The HP Way: How Bill Hewlett and I Built Our Company* (New York: HarperBusiness, 1995), pp. 112–113.

David Packard

HEWLETT-PACKARD

Craftsmen

> Capability
> Pride in One's Work
> Quality .
> Trusting People

Hire the right people and you'll be surprised at the results. In order to maximize efficiency and achieve success, David Packard says it's absolutely critical to hire the most capable people for the job. Once there, they should be treated with consideration and respect and their accomplishments should be celebrated. Creating the right environment for people to do their best is critical. Details are particularly important in Packard's business and can spell the difference between a quality product and a failure.

Packard tells of a time when he was following his management philosophy of MBWA ("management by walking around") and was strolling around a machine shop. He happened upon a machinist who was in the middle of making a plastic mold die. The machinist had apparently been working on perfecting it and was polishing and making a final cut. Packard says that without thinking, he reached down and wiped it with his finger. The machinist was irate. "Get your finger off my mold!" he scolded him. His manager, embarrassed at the situation, upbraided the machinist, lecturing him that he had no idea whom he was talking to, etc. *"I don't care!"* the machinist shot back. Far from being upset, Packard told him he was absolutely right. The machinist had an important job to do. Packard was interrupting someone who was taking pride in doing it right. He should have known better.

Using This Anecdote

In creative companies, rank should not matter as much as results and pride in one's work. Packard's story is a great reminder of how superior "management by objective" is compared with "management by org chart." Try this: "We need to remember that titles in this company don't mean much if you are not adding value to the company. We need to trust professionals to be professionals. There's a story David Packard tells . . ."

Source
David Packard, *The HP Way: How Bill Hewlett and I Built Our Company* (New York: HarperBusiness, 1995), p. 127.

David Packard

HEWLETT-PACKARD

"Call Me David . . ."

> Human Resources
> Communication
> Open Management

HP didn't have an HR department in its early years. Hard as it seems to believe, Bill Hewlett and David Packard operated the first eighteen years of HP without a human resources department. Didn't need one, they reasoned. Perhaps the company's spectacular growth eventually forced the change. Packard says it wasn't that they had any particular aversion to personnel managers; it's just that they thought such a department would get in the way of deepening the relationship between employees and management.

Another feature that Packard says distinguishes HP is its informality and the openness of communications. First names are always used instead of more formal greetings. Org charts, while a necessary management feature, should play no role when it comes to the individual employee getting his or her work done. Packard says they want employees to communicate with one another "guided by common sense rather than by the lines and box on an org chart." To get his or her tasks completed, he says, "an individual is expected to seek information from the most likely source."

Using This Anecdote

The mere fact that HP didn't have an HR department for nearly the first two decades of its existence is probably noteworthy enough to mention in a speech. Not many companies can say that. Successful communications today should not be hierarchical but purpose driven. Try this: "We need to be less driven by org charts and more driven by focusing on getting the job done. Hard as it is to believe, HP started out without a major department for nearly twenty years after it was founded . . ."

Source
David Packard, *The HP Way: How Bill Hewlett and I Built Our Company* (New York: HarperBusiness, 1995), pp. 158–159.

David Packard

HEWLETT-PACKARD

No More Lock and Key

> Access to Equipment
> Innovation
> Trust

Just return it . . . David Packard says early in his career when he worked at GE, the company at the time was zealous about guarding property that it thought employees would walk off with and not return. What made this policy especially difficult for innovators and tinkerers like Packard was the fact that many of these tools were useful in informal experimentations after hours. He says the fact that they locked it all up served as a provocation to walk off with equipment anyway. And that's just what some people did. He adds that at one point there was actually so much "borrowed" equipment in the attic of one house where a number of employees were living that when they threw the switch, the streetlights outside actually dimmed!

When they founded HP, he and Bill Hewlett decided to ignore that rule. But someone apparently didn't get the memo. In one story, Packard tells of a time when Hewlett went to the plant one weekend to do some work and stopped by to pick up a microscope in the company storeroom, only to find a locked equipment cage. Since he didn't have the key, he decided to break open the latch and left a note saying to never leave the equipment locked like that again. Denying access to equipment wasn't just a potential break in innovation, it was signaling a lack of trust, and that had to be stopped.

Using This Anecdote

If you work with professionals and you can't trust them, then perhaps you hired the wrong people. This story is a good one for reminding people that where there is no trust, professionals will rebel. Try this: "This company was built on trust. We are all professionals and I know I can trust you to adapt to this new change we're implementing. I am reminded of a story David Packard tells . . ."

Source

David Packard, *The HP Way: How Bill Hewlett and I Built Our Company* (New York: HarperBusiness, 1995), pp. 135–137.

David Packard

HEWLETT-PACKARD

Caveat Emptor

> Acquisitions
> Buyer's Remorse

Don't bite off more than you can chew. David Packard says he and cofounder Bill Hewlett didn't want to see HP become a conglomerate. He jokes that when it comes to buying other companies, more companies have died from indigestion than from starvation. He says their first acquisition was in the late 1950s, of a company in Pasadena, California. It was a good fit, and the founder later served as a member of HP's managing board. It would be the first of many acquisitions helping HP enter new markets and expand offerings.

But not every acquisition worked. More often than not, corporate culture differences stood in the way. Packard tells the story of a company HP acquired in the mid-1960s called Autodynamics. The company made equipment that used ultrasonic energy to find flaws in metals. Packard says one of their products was called "Mustang." He noticed that at the center of each piece of the equipment, they had apparently taken a metal car badge from a Ford Mustang—which was a new model at the time—and tried to pass it off as their own. He says it didn't exactly inspire confidence. Nor did finding out about contracts they previously hadn't mentioned but which still had to be honored, as well as faulty equipment. Although HP fulfilled the contracts, after eight months the entire operation was shut down.

Using This Anecdote

Most growing companies have either made—or thought about making—acquisitions. But like marriages, not all of them end up happily ever after. A warning or two ahead of time could be good advice. Try this: "I know we've expressed an interest in acquiring one or several companies. But I caution everyone here to remember that most mergers fail. David Packard tells an interesting story about one acquisition HP made . . ."

Source

David Packard, *The HP Way: How Bill Hewlett and I Built Our Company* (New York: HarperBusiness, 1995), pp. 142–144.

David Packard

HEWLETT-PACKARD

Employees Choose Their Leaders

> Earning Respect
> Leadership
> Management Potential

Respect is earned, not given. David Packard says that when he and Bill Hewlett were watching their small start-up grow into a much bigger company, they could no longer take teamwork for granted. The organization had to be *managed*. He says they did not want their company to be a "hire-and-fire" operation where people were brought in for short-term contracts and then let go once the task was accomplished. They thought much more long term and focused instead on a dedicated and stable workforce.

Part of that equation involved identifying from within their ranks those who had management potential. Packard tells the story of how they once promoted a worker to be the manager of their machine shop. The promotion made sense since both Packard and Hewlett saw him as a good worker, and the move was seen as a step up for him. A few days later, however, the newly appointed manager came to see Packard in his office. He explained that he wasn't having an easy time in his new position. He then asked if Packard could come out to the shop and make it clear to his team that he was indeed their boss. Packard looked at him and said, "If I have to do that, you don't deserve to be their boss."

Using This Anecdote

Although a boss may be thrust upon his or her direct reports, it doesn't mean that individual will be respected. That respect must be earned. It really is true—employees decide whom they trust to lead them. If the "leader" has to go to his or her boss to impose control, it's game over. Try this: "Managers cannot lead by coercion; they must lead by example and they must earn the trust of those who report to them. David Packard tells the story . . ."

Source

David Packard, *The HP Way: How Bill Hewlett and I Built Our Company* (New York: HarperBusiness, 1995), pp. 128–129.

> Bureaucracy
> Centralization vs. Decentralization
> Decision-Making Paralysis
> Organization

That which expands can also contract. Like many companies in high-growth businesses, as Hewlett-Packard grew it created countless layers of divisions, task forces, committees, councils, etc. For a major player in the computer business that often needs to turn on a dime, it was rapidly turning into a nightmare. Important decisions requiring immediate attention were often tabled for weeks, sometimes months, because of bureaucratic inertia. By 1990, it had reached a crisis point. Just as the company was entering the computer business, the company was not responding quickly enough to make necessary decisions. This soon began to affect other parts of the business. Responding to the problem, the company formed the Computer Business Executive Committee, with the intention of focusing decisions and coordinating computer activities. That, too, didn't work.

The paralysis only got worse and the stock started falling to $25 by

1990, after having broken $70 as little as three years earlier. By this time, both Packard and Hewlett were retired. But they weren't totally out of the picture. Luckily, the company's open-door policy gave them a line into current employees frustrated by the paralysis. Their advice was simple: Reduce the number of layers of management, bring in a new chief executive, and disband the Computer Business Executive Committee. Operating units were given greater freedom to plan their business and make decisions on their own. The result was a more flexible company. Three years later, the swing back to decentralization was already making a difference. Customers responded. By 1993, the stock had doubled back to $70.

Using This Anecdote

Bureaucracy is the enemy in any company—especially those needing to turn on a dime. And few industries need to be as agile as the computer business, where change is often the only constant. Luckily for HP, they identified the problem, fixed it, and survived. Try this: "As managers, we should acknowledge that the answer to many problems is not to form a committee to overcome our challenges, but to empower our people to make decisions. We're doing just that. David Packard tells the story at Hewlett-Packard . . ."

Source
David Packard, *The HP Way: How Bill Hewlett and I Built Our Company* (New York: HarperBusiness, 1995), pp. 148–150.

HEWLETT-PACKARD

"Don't Mind Me, I'm Just Watching . . ."

> Attention to Detail
> Management by Walking Around (MBWA)
> Quality

The devil is in the details. David Packard tells the story of an incident that occurred early in his career when he was working at GE. His division was having problems with vacuum tubes (remember, this was a long time ago, in the 1930s). Batch after batch had failed quality inspections, and Packard was assigned to find the root cause. To understand the situation better, he spent more time on the factory floor retracing the entire process. After a while, he started noticing something. The written instructions on how to manufacture the product, provided by the manufacturer, were often far from accurate. He then worked with the people on the line to rewrite the document so they had the proper instructions going forward. It paid off. Every single tube in the next batch passed muster.

Years later, Packard remembered this incident, particularly when he and Bill Hewlett were developing the management policies for HP. It was what inspired their adoption of "management by walking around" (MBWA). "I learned that quality requires minute attention to every detail, that everyone in an organization wants to do a good job, that written instructions are seldom adequate, and that personal involvement is essential," he says.

Using This Anecdote

It's the small things that matter. For managers, that means staying on top of what goes on in their shop, not being distant and removed. Try this: "We all talk about the need to maintain quality, but I want to remind everyone here that unless you're personally involved, we're going to continue having quality issues. David Packard tells the story . . ."

Source

David Packard, *The HP Way: How Bill Hewlett and I Built Our Company* (New York: HarperBusiness, 1995), pp. 155–156.

Larry Page

GOOGLE

Present at the Creation

> Experimenting
> Eureka Moment
> Meeting a Need
> Search Engine

Google started as a lark. Cofounder Larry Page says that when he was a student at Stanford University he started collecting links on the World Wide Web with no intention of creating a search engine. He was essentially curious about which pages were linked to which pages—something few if any people were looking into in the mid-1990s. If anything, Page thought this might lead to a topic for his dissertation paper and be fun to do at the same time. Little did he know it would eventually make him a billionaire.

He says he started by finding out who was linked to Stanford University's home page. At the time, there were about ten thousand links. The problem then was sorting through all the results to figure out which were the most relevant. So Page developed a way to rank the links based on the links themselves. The results he got were essentially what he had expected—minus the extraneous information. Simply put, instead of drowning in a sea of ten thousand links, he got the top ten results he had intuitively expected all along. He says he thought to himself, "This is really interesting. This really works. We should use it for search." Eureka. It was at that point that along with Sergey Brin he started building in earnest the search engine that would soon become the industry gold standard. The rest, as they say, is history.

Using This Anecdote

More than a few great ideas have come from raw experimentation with no specific direction in mind. Perhaps it's the freedom. Perhaps it's the fact that there are no great expectations. Try this: "I hope we can come up with a great solution. To help get you thinking in a more creative direction, I can't help but mention that many great ideas throughout history came from trying to solve one challenge in one area and ending up creating opportunities in another. In some cases, this has even led to the creation of multibillion-dollar businesses. I'm reminded of a story Google founder Larry Page tells . . ."

Source
Academy of Achievement, "Making the World's Information Accessible," October 28, 2000, London: www.achievement.org/autodoc/page/pag0int-1.

> Age
> America
> Generational Bet
> Opportunity

Opportunity in a country like the United States is simply too irresistible. Billionaire energy financier T. Boone Pickens tells the story of being asked to address his grandson's high school graduating class in 2007. As his speech began, he already knew most people had one thing on their mind: When is this guy going to wrap it up so we can all go to lunch? Pickens then told the audience something that grabbed their attention. He told them they had the best seat in the house when it came to opportunities ahead and that he would trade everything he had to be in their place. He then recited a long list of assets he had, including his Gulfstream jet, his sixty-thousand-acre ranch, etc.

"There's only one catch," he added coyly. "If you make the trade, you have to be seventy-nine and I get to be eighteen again." Now he *really* had their attention. Some students gamely asked about his plane, his ranch, and the other assets he mentioned. But in the end, there were *no* takers. He says it would have been a great deal for him, but a lousy one for any of the young graduates. Knowing he can't change his age, Pickens says the next best thing is to stay active and engaged no matter how old—life deserves second, third, even fourth acts. He adds that a journalist once asked him why he didn't step aside so a younger person could have his turn. He says that image of a small feeding trough is wrong. "Everyone can step up," he says. "All you have to do is work hard and take advantage of the opportunities you're given."

Using This Anecdote

He doesn't mention it, but it's pretty safe to assume that when Pickens made that bet with the audience, you probably could have heard a pin drop. Despite being offered immense wealth, no one would dare trade it in for his or her youth and the opportunities that lay ahead in their own lives. Opportunity is at the core of this country's promise. You may not always succeed, but you at least have the chance. Try this: "Sometimes we have a tendency to forget the power opportunity holds for us. I'm reminded of a story T. Boone Pickens told . . ."

Source
T. Boone Pickens, *The First Billion Is the Hardest* (New York: Crown Business, 2008), pp. 248–249.

T. Boone Pickens

BP CAPITAL MANAGEMENT

Second Acts—Third Time's a Charm

> Failing
> Test Taking
> Licensing
> Mental Arithmetic
> Second Acts

Second acts are often more interesting than first ones. And T. Boone Pickens has had more than his share of second acts in life. In one instance in 1996, Pickens founded BP Capital Energy Fund after already having had a very lucrative career in the oil business. But he tells the story of how, to become a licensed commodities pool operator, he needed to pass the National Futures Association exam. At this point in his career, he had launched his business, and two of his traders had already passed the exam on their first try. How hard could the test be? Pickens boned up on the subject, studied hard, then went to take the exam. A young man in the testing room recognized him and asked Pickens what he was doing there. He joked that he thought Pickens had written the book on the subject, much less didn't need to take the test! Pickens then took up the entire six hours allotted for the exam. He passed the first part, but failed the other two. No license. He then redoubled his efforts. This time, he hired a tutor and took the test a second time. But once again, he flunked.

His apprenticeship was taking far longer than he'd thought it would. He then went to bat for a third time. This time around, though, he took colleagues' advice and ditched the calculator. He was used to doing mental arithmetic in the office anyhow. Before starting the exam, he asked the instructor—the same one who had seen him flunk two times before—whether he could get all day to take the test. The instructor said he would ask his headquarters in Kansas City only if he failed this time. Boone took the exam, handed in his papers, and waited. The instructor then had a broad grin on her face. "We don't have to call Kansas City after all," she announced. "You passed."

Using This Anecdote

Talk about humbling. By 1996, T. Boone Pickens was already a well-known figure in the oil business, having graced the cover of more than a few business magazines. Now, in a new business for him, he failed to get the credentials he needed. Perhaps it was letting go of the calculator, perhaps it was just sheer persistence—whatever the cause, he finally succeeded. Try this: "Sometimes second acts, even for those wildly successful in their first act, don't come easily. I'm reminded of a story T. Boone Pickens tells . . ."

Source
T. Boone Pickens, *The First Billion Is the Hardest* (New York: Crown Business, 2008), pp. 66–68.

T. Boone Pickens

BP CAPITAL MANAGEMENT

Lucky Shoes

> Frugality
> Cheapness
> Lucky Charm
> Acting Like an Owner

Call it a good-luck talisman. T. Boone Pickens says he grew up with frugality in his family and has kept the trait ever since. He remembers his grandmother scolding him for leaving the lights on, then showing him the next electric bill to prove to him how much his mistake cost. He says he has habitually been turning out the lights when leaving rooms ever since.

Among some of the possessions he says he still hangs on to today are a Rolex watch bought in 1964 in Vienna (maxing out two credit cards with that purchase); a bird-shaped silver pillbox bought in 1959; and a pair of resoled penny loafers bought in 1957. The loafers have a special history since he says he almost lost them along a California freeway years ago. At the time, he was on a family vacation and had the luggage strapped to the roof of their station wagon. One problem, though. He forgot to zip the case. All of a sudden, while looking in the rearview mirror, Pickens saw his clothes being strewn wildly across the freeway. He quickly realized what was happening, slowed down, and pulled over to the side of the road. Traffic was whirring by—not exactly an ideal situation to walk out onto the busy road. He told his wife that he thought he could get everything in two trips. His son got on the floor, fearful his father would be hit. Pickens ran out, gathered everything he could—including the shoes—packed again and continued driving. He says he even wears those same shoes occasionally. "I sometimes think they're lucky," he says. "And when things aren't going so well, I wear them." Whatever works.

Using This Anecdote

It's never a bad habit to watch your money like a hawk, whether it's small personal items or billions of dollars that belong to shareholders. And more than a few businesspeople have personal talismans that bring them luck—at least they believe so. Try this: "Frugality is a virtue in my opinion. Many of the most successful businesspeople— and businesses—run a very tight ship. I remember a story T. Boone Pickens told . . ."

Source
T. Boone Pickens, *The First Billion Is the Hardest* (New York: Crown Business, 2008), pp. 21–22.

T. Boone Pickens

BP CAPITAL MANAGEMENT

Don't Ever Forget Who Owns the Place

> Dividend
> Right Sizing
> Responding to Market Realities
> Shareholders

It was music to shareholders' ears. T. Boone Pickens tells a story he heard about a directors' meeting at a rival oil company many years ago. A member of the board whose family founded the company had proposed increasing the annual dividend. The CEO was, well . . . of a different opinion. According to Pickens, he answered the board member by saying, "Have you lost your goddamned mind? Why would we give people we don't know a bunch of money?" According to Pickens, this was typical of the attitude of corporate America toward shareholders during the 1970s and earlier. Although Pickens's own company, Mesa, had been doing well, he said it was getting increasingly hard to replace its oil reserves, despite having done so for eighteen years straight. Pickens says he was intent on growing the company, but there were fewer opportunities to find oil.

Clearly, he would need to significantly increase his exploration and development budget. The result, though, would be increasingly thinner margins. He then gave a speech saying that if the company failed to replace its reserves for two years in a row, he'd either figure out a different approach or exit the business altogether. Then it dawned on him: He could make Mesa smaller and then spin off some of the reserves to shareholders in a royalty trust. The result was the oil and gas properties they owned would be smaller, making it relatively easier to get replacement reserves. In other words, although the company would become smaller, shareholder value would increase. Sure enough, Mesa was at $54 a share when the royalty was announced. By the time the trust was approved a few months later, it was at $86. The move later became a trend with other companies. Pickens never forgot who actually owned the company.

Using This Anecdote

It sounds counterintuitive, but sometimes you have to shed parts of a company to increase value. It certainly made sense for Pickens's shareholders, who would have seen their stock plummet in the face of depleting reserves. Try this: "Our company is actually worth less growing than it could be worth by divesting. T. Boone Pickens tells a similar story from years ago with his oil company, Mesa . . ."

Source
T. Boone Pickens, *The First Billion Is the Hardest* (New York: Crown Business, 2008), pp. 22–23.

T. Boone Pickens

BP CAPITAL MANAGEMENT

"You Mean You're the 'Team'?"

> Hedge Fund
> Human Capital
> Lean Management
> Organizational Size

Just because a company is big does not mean it is well run. Or that it has vision. In fact, according to T. Boone Pickens, more often than not, the exact opposite is true. He makes the point that you can't judge a company by the number of its employees. For example, the greater the distance and isolation between senior management and the line business, the more that distance leads to complacency and the more it saps creative energy. He says he always worked shorthanded at his oil company, Mesa. And the same is true at BP Capital.

He tells the story of the youngest member of his BP staff, David Meaney. Meaney had started trading stocks and bonds in his senior year at college. After getting a finance degree and working seven years as a sales and portfolio trader, he wanted to switch over to an energy-related hedge fund. Hearing of BP's success, he sent them his résumé. At the interview, Meaney said he was eager to join the team at BP Capital.

The person interviewing him, Michael Ross, said, "Well, there's only one trader—me." Meaney then asked, "You guys are managing four and a half billion dollars and you have only one trader?" Yup. Sure enough, Meaney was hired, and the number of traders doubled to the astronomical two. Size, indeed, isn't everything.

Using This Anecdote

Sometimes smaller is beautiful. But it also needs to be to scale. When the job can be done with a few talented people instead of a cast of thousands, all the better. Try this: "I've heard many arguments that we should start hiring, as if that alone will make us more productive. More bureaucracy and more layers of management are not always the answer. Some companies do just fine as lean organizations. I'm reminded of a story T. Boone Pickens tells of his $4.5 billion energy hedge fund . . ."

Source
T. Boone Pickens, *The First Billion Is the Hardest* (New York: Crown Business, 2008), pp. 22–23.

T. Boone Pickens

BP CAPITAL MANAGEMENT

The Wind's Blowing This Way...

> Not in My Backyard (NIMBY)
> Reverse Psychology
> Siting
> Wind Turbines

T. Boone Pickens always seems to know which way the wind is blowing. The former oilman made headlines when he announced he was entering the wind power business. His home state of Texas not only has huge oil reserves, it's also part of America's so-called wind corridor stretching from Texas all the way north to the border with Canada. The Texas Panhandle in particular is known for especially windy conditions. Pickens says, for example, that a 640-acre area of land can support up to five to ten wind turbines, each of which can generate somewhere between $10,000 and $30,000 annually in royalties to landowners. For a part of the state that has been losing population, that kind of income can be a nice incentive to stay, which helps spur local economic development.

Still, people have to be convinced to lease their land. And they have to be convinced in large enough numbers for a large investment to make any sense. Pickens tells the story of meeting with some two hundred people, some of whom already knew Pickens from a deal he had made for water rights. Now he was trying to get them to sell him their wind. He doesn't say so explicitly, but it appears he tried a little bit of reverse psychology on the group. Opening the session, he says, he wanted everybody in the room to know that he didn't want wind turbines on his own property. "Why?" someone asked. "Because they're ugly," Boone answered. A person in the front row then said, "I don't see that well. They may be ugly to Boone, but they look like money to me!" That line got a big laugh, and the sale, according to Pickens, was an easy one after that.

Using This Anecdote

Sometimes the best way to deal with resistance is to use a dose of reverse psychology that gets right to the heart of personal interests. By acknowledging that the turbines aren't exactly beautiful—a NIMBY argument many have made elsewhere—Pickens took the debate away from aesthetics and shifted it toward other interests. Try this: "We need to shift the debate on locating this plant. No, it will not likely win a lot of awards for architectural beauty, but it will create jobs. I remember a story T. Boone Pickens once told about getting people to lease their land for wind turbines . . ."

Source
T. Boone Pickens, *The First Billion Is the Hardest* (New York: Crown Business, 2008), pp. 231–233.

Jim Sinegal

COSTCO WHOLESALE CORPORATION

"Attention, Customers, CEO in Aisle Five . . ."

> Teaching
> Leading by Example
> Attention to Details

Actions often speak far louder than words. Costco Wholesale cofounder and CEO Jim Sinegal says that some of the best advice he ever got wasn't actually "advice" in the traditional sense of the word. He tells a story of when he was a young executive at a discount retailer and what he learned from Sol Price, the company's founder. Sinegal says Sol was the consummate teacher who preferred to lead by example. He says that even after dinner, Sol would come back to the warehouse and walk up and down the aisles looking everything over with his eagle eye.

If he saw garbage on the floor, he'd pick it up. If something had tipped over, he'd put it right side up. If a display was uneven, he'd fix it. If something wasn't being attended to, he'd make sure it was done. More to the point, he would show people how things should be done—so they would learn by doing, learn by example. That lesson stuck with Sinegal who, as CEO of Costco himself, is also always working the floors and asking employees about their daily tasks. That lesson is with him all these years later: To be a really effective manager, you should also be a good teacher who leads by example, with actions speaking louder than words.

Using This Anecdote

Good habits picked up early in life can help later in life. This story also shows that the best leaders lead by example, not just words alone. Attention to little details like the shop display may not seem like a big deal, but it becomes infectious as others follow the example. When they do, the whole company benefits. Try this: "It's the little things that count in business just like they do in life. The head of Costco, for example, learned this lesson very early in his career . . ."

Source
Mina Kimes, "Best Advice I Ever Got," *Fortune*, July 8, 2009: http://money
.cnn.com/galleries/2009/fortune/0906/gallery.best_advice_i_ever_got2
.fortune/2.html.

Donald Trump

THE TRUMP ORGANIZATION

A Chip Off the Old Block—Sort Of

> Family Profession
> Father-Son Relations
> Frugality
> High Margins vs. Low Margins

Like father, not exactly like son. Donald Trump entered his father's business—real estate—but didn't follow exactly in his father's footsteps. His dad, Fred Trump, had built lower- to middle-income housing throughout New York City's outer boroughs. "The Donald" loved the real estate business but was turned off by some of the downsides of his dad's slice of the real estate market. In one story, he tells how his father's business was a little too rough for this freshly minted Wharton business school grad. Newly employed by his father, young Don was assigned to go around with rent collectors. One of the tricks he says he learned was never stand in front of the door when knocking. Stand, instead, to the side, so the only thing in harm's way would be your hand, for safety.

The other part of the business he didn't like was the low margins. In his dad's segment of the business, he says, there was no choice but to pinch pennies. In many of his buildings, for example, they used red

brick because it was a penny cheaper than tan bricks. Not much empha-
sis was placed on design, and a few bucks saved here and there could spell
the difference between making a profit—or not. Trump tells the story of
his father visiting the building of Trump Tower at 57th Street and Fifth
Avenue in Manhattan. As the tower was going up, Trump says they were
using bronze solar glass—far more expensive than any form of brick. His
father looked at the construction under way and told Donald, "Why
don't you forget the damn glass? Give them four or five stories of it and
then use common brick for the rest. No one's going to look up anyway."
It was a turning point: a father looking to give advice to his up-and-
coming son on saving a few dollars, and a son now more convinced than
ever that he made the right decision to pursue loftier dreams than his
dad. The younger Trump knew the more expensive material meant a
different kind of owner/tenant than his father was used to dealing with
and the chance to make higher margins. Although grateful for his dad's
advice, he nonetheless continued on a different path.

Using This Anecdote

Times change and so do generational ambitions. Drawn to his father's
business, but not drawn to everything his father encountered—the
rough edges, the low margins—Trump set out on a different path.
Try this: "Our customers are on the higher end of the market, so we
need to migrate there. That's also where the higher margins are. I'm
reminded of a story Donald Trump told about his dad, Fred, whom
he followed into the real estate business . . ."

Source
Donald J. Trump, *The Art of the Deal* (New York: Random House, 1987),
pp. 54–55.

> Deal Making
> Downside Risk
> Conservative Business Approach
> Patience

Although he owns casinos, Donald Trump says he's not much of a gambler. In fact, he says he takes a pretty conservative approach to business deals. He says he's a believer actually in the power of negative thinking. "If you plan for the worst—if you can live with the worst—the good will always take care of itself," he says. As a result, Trump says that he tries to never leave himself too exposed in any deal. He cites the story of buying a losing USFL football team as one example where he didn't follow his own rules and paid the price.

In a more typical example, he tells the story of building along the boardwalk in Atlantic City. He had patiently put together a number of deals on parcels of land contingent on him being able to assemble the entire site. Once the site was consolidated, he did not rush to construct the building. Yes, letting the site sit idle cost money. But on the other hand, he wanted to be absolutely certain he had won his gaming license from the state of New Jersey, so his exposure was lower. Along came Holiday Inn, offering a 50 percent cut in the deal in return for paying for all the construction plus guaranteeing him against losses for five years. Hilton, by contrast, moved much quicker than Trump, simultaneously filing for a gaming license and beginning construction on a separate $400 million site. Just two months before the hotel was to open, Hilton was denied its gaming license and was forced to sell to Trump under enormous pressure. Trump then renamed the facility "Trump's Castle." Patience can indeed be a virtue.

Using This Anecdote

The old story about the tortoise beating the hare is not necessarily apocryphal in the world of business. Speed is important, but so is intelligently leveraging against risk. In this case, Trump correctly saw huge downside risk in moving too fast without his gaming license. His competitor took way too much risk and ended up losing badly. Try this: "We all know the story of the tortoise and the hare. It actually explains a lot of our own strategy as to why we may seem cautious, when in fact we're being prudent. Here's an example from Donald Trump . . ."

Source
Donald J. Trump, *The Art of the Deal* (New York: Random House, 1987), pp. 34–35.

Donald Trump

THE TRUMP ORGANIZATION

Save the Money You Spend on Consultants

> Consulting Firms
> Marketing Surveys
> Saving Money
> Knowing Your Audience

It costs nothing to ask. Donald Trump says he greatly admires those who have a sense of the market they work in. He counts among those who have an innate sense of their respective markets Steven Spielberg, Lee Iaccoca, Woody Allen, and Sylvester Stallone. Each knows what his public wants and each delivers. Trump says he adds himself to that list and takes pride in the fact that he doesn't hire a lot of number crunchers. Nor does he trust fancy marketing surveys. For example, he says consulting firms will send a group down from Boston, rent expensive hotel rooms, and then charge you a sum well into the six figures for a study that usually has no conclusion and often takes so long to complete that the deal has long since come and gone.

Trump says he's instead a great believer in doing his own research. He'll ask his sources what they think of a property he's considering buying. He says he'll go out to the neighborhood and ask around what people think of the area in terms of schools, safety, shopping, etc. If he's buying a property in another city, he makes a point to talk to cabbies, waiters, and others he comes in contact with. As he puts it, "I ask and I ask and I ask, until I begin to get a gut feeling about something. And that's when I make a decision."

Using This Anecdote

Trump may be a little harsh on consultants, but he's dead right on using your instinct and asking, asking, asking. No serious decision should be made without doing your homework, knowing your market. Are your own people doing exactly what Trump says he does? Are they asking the questions from people who really know? Try this: "We can hire all the fancy consultants in the world, but I have a feeling we'd be wasting our money in the end. What we need are eyes and ears on the ground. I'm reminded of how Donald Trump gathers some of his research . . ."

Source
Donald J. Trump, *The Art of the Deal* (New York: Random House, 1987), pp. 36–37.

> Negotiating
> Finding the Real Decision Maker
> Organizational Politics
> Sealing a Deal

Not getting the answer you want? Take it to the next level. When Donald Trump was in the midst of buying the failing Commodore Hotel next to Grand Central Terminal in New York City, he was negotiating to get the Hyatt hotel chain to locate its flagship New York hotel on the site. He says he had negotiated a deal with a Hyatt executive that was full of contingencies. Proud of himself, he nonetheless saw the deal eventually fall through. He renegotiated and shook hands, only to see the same pattern of failure emerge again and again. Finally, someone higher up in the Hyatt organization whom Trump had befriended gave the then young real estate developer some friendly advice: He should see Jay Pritzker, whose family had a controlling interest in the hotel chain. His source added something else—Pritzker was the guy who *actually* ran the company.

As Trump says, "It comes down to the fact that everyone underneath the top guy is just an employee [and] an employee isn't going to fight for your deal." He'll fight for a raise, or a bonus, but the last thing he wants to do is upset the boss. He's more than likely to present your deal with no opinion. To you, he might sound enthusiastic, but that enthusiasm fades quickly when he goes to his boss and states your case. It's often not worth the risk for an employee. Trump says he picked up the phone and called Pritzker himself. Turns out Pritzker was on his way from Chicago to New York and said they should meet. Trump picked him up at the airport and they talked while Pritzker was in the city. While both men played their cards close to the vest, a mutual respect grew between the two. Before long, they had a deal: Trump would build the hotel, Hyatt would manage it, and they'd both be equal partners. Lesson learned: None of this would have been possible without eventually going to the boss.

Using This Anecdote

It pays sometimes to go straight to the top. Trump learned the hard way that what he thought were well-negotiated deals were not to be so long as they didn't have the right political backing. Intermediaries may be enthusiastic in shaking your hand on a deal, but don't expect them to carry that enthusiasm to their own boss. They have their own personal agenda to worry about. Try this: "When it comes to sales, I'm noticing that we are indeed getting in the door, but we're not sealing the deal. I can only think that one thing is happening here. We're not going high enough up the ladder. I'm reminded of a story Donald Trump tells . . ."

Source
Donald J. Trump, *The Art of the Deal* (New York: Random House, 1987), p. 86.

> Personal Touch
> Creative Negotiating
> Thinking Outside the Box

It was an early lesson in business psychology. Media mogul Ted Turner recounts a story from his younger days of working in the leasing department of his father's booming billboard business throughout the South. The job entailed convincing people to lease land that had the best advantages for putting up a billboard: a good line of sight and lots of traffic. The owner would then get an annual payment in exchange for letting the company use the land. Turner writes that many of the sales were tough. But no single individual was as tough to convince as one particular woman in Savannah, Georgia. Years before, developers had given up on trying to buy her out and ended up building a Sears Roebuck around her, with her house now standing in the middle of a parking lot! When Turner prepared to ask her to allow them to put up a billboard, he knew ahead of time whom he was up against. This tough, stubborn widow had already refused a large cash settlement to move, so why would she accept a much smaller offer to put up a billboard? Undaunted, Turner made it his mission to convince her.

Try after try didn't work. After offering a compromise that would have had the billboard cover only the second-floor windows of her house, she still refused. Then it dawned on him. After visiting her home during a particularly sweltering summer, he realized how hot it was inside her house, especially with her home situated in the middle of an asphalt parking lot! He then discussed with his father an idea he had and went back to the woman with a deal sweetener. In addition to the original fee, the company was willing to buy and install an air conditioner for her. No one had thought of it before. Touched by his thoughtfulness, she accepted Turner's deal. The billboard went up and Turner got a lesson in negotiations he's carried with him since.

Using This Anecdote

Great negotiators think creatively. What box? The right answer in negotiations is not always more money. Sometimes the right answer is putting yourself in the shoes of the other person, understanding what their true needs and motivations are, then trying to meet them halfway. Try this: "I know it's been tough getting deals lately, but let me tell you a story I think shows how we need to think more out of the box . . ."

Source
Ted Turner, *Call Me Ted* (New York: Grand Central Publishing, 2008), pp. 44–45.

Ted Turner

TURNER ENTERPRISES

One Expensive Drink

> Accounting
> Amortization
> Betting
> Father-Son Relations

Amortization is not exactly a scintillating topic. But Ted Turner sure enough spins a good yarn on the subject. He says many years ago he made a bet with his father—an alcoholic and two-pack-a-day smoker—that while a sophomore at Brown University he could avoid smoking and alcohol before his twenty-first birthday. If he did this, his father promised to pay him $5,000—a princely sum back in the 1950s. His father also agreed to send him a very small allowance as long as he wrote weekly letters to him updating him on campus life.

At one point, he missed writing to his dad two weeks in a row and his allowance was suspended. Then, just after turning nineteen, he gave in to temptation and got drunk for the first time, smoking his first cigar to boot! He knew he had broken his promise to his father. An honest kid, he told his dad. His father was furious at the news and canceled the $5,000 deal. Disappointed, but not surprised, a philosophical young Ted Turner decided to apply the principles of amortization he had learned while working at his father's business. By his calculation, that first drink cost him $5,000. The second drink brought the cost down to $2,500. The next five drinks would be $1,000, and so on. By that same stretch of logic, he reckoned that if he had five thousand drinks over the coming years, it would only cost him $1 a drink. *That* he could afford!

Using This Anecdote

This story can be used to bring a little levity to a relatively dry topic. Turner's story is a great way to illustrate just that, while also demonstrating humility on Turner's part. After all, he *was* honest about breaking his promise when he could have just as easily never told his dad the truth. Try this: "We've got to take full advantage of all the accounting rules at our disposal, including things like amortization. That reminds me of a story I read about from Ted Turner's early years . . ."

Source
Ted Turner, *Call Me Ted* (New York: Grand Central Publishing, 2008), pp. 29–30.

Ted Turner

TURNER ENTERPRISES

Hoist the Mainsail

> Management Philosophy
> Delegating Authority
> Entrepreneurs Dealing with Growth

Maybe it's the salt air . . . An avid sailor and America's Cup winner, Ted Turner says that part of his passion for efficiency in business stems from his love of sailing. Shaving a second or two off your time can spell the difference between victory and defeat. He writes that racing has long been a metaphor for how he runs his business, especially as an entrepreneur. He says the small things matter. And as you graduate from smaller to bigger boats, the size of the crew grows, and so, too, does the need to manage them. No one person can do it all.

As the skipper of the boat, you're in charge of figuring out the strategy, plotting the course, and issuing the orders. It's not much different in business. He says that you have to find the right people and let them do their jobs, while keeping an eye on the overall strategy. This is especially a problem for entrepreneurs who watch their companies grow. Because they're so used to running everything on their own, entrepreneurs sometimes have a hard time letting go. They need to learn how to trust and delegate—just like skippering a winning high-performance sailboat. "I stayed on top of the key issues related to our individual business, but I let my managers manage," he writes. "This gave me time to focus on the big picture."

Using This Anecdote

One of managers' key functions is to trust and delegate. No one can possibly do everything well. That's why you hire the best people for the job in the first place. But you also have to trust them to execute. Try this: "I think we have to stop micromanaging here. Managers in your position should be dealing with the business at a much more strategic level. Ted Turner likens business managers to the captain of a boat—and he knows a thing or two about both . . ."

Source
Ted Turner, *Call Me Ted* (New York: Grand Central Publishing, 2008), p. 261.

Ted Turner

TURNER ENTERPRISES

"Rosebud . . ."

> Ambition
> Beating the Odds
> Setting Goals

Some generations are luckier than others. Media mogul Ted Turner tells the story of his father's early years. His dad, Robert Edward "Ed" Turner, was clearly ambitious and driven as a young man, and he had been accepted into Duke University just as the Great Depression hit. Ed's parents nearly lost everything—like a lot of Americans—during that difficult period, and they were devastated at having to tell their son they couldn't afford the tuition. Ed Turner didn't let himself feel defeated, however. He understood the circumstances and reassured his mother, telling her that everything was going to be all right. He was going to succeed no matter what. He was going to become a millionaire, have a big house, and buy a yacht.

Given the fact that the Great Depression had just begun and the U.S. economy was in tatters, this sounded more like wishful thinking than a realistic prospect. But by the time Ted Turner had heard this story from his dad, his father had actually made good on all three promises—without exception! His father said, however, that while he had checked off all three, he was now having a tough time coming up with a plan for the rest of his life. The lesson, he told Ted, was that it is better to set your goals so high that you'll never likely achieve them all. That way there will always be something to shoot for. "I made the mistake of setting my goals too low," Ted quotes his father as saying, "and now I have a hard time coming up with new ones." Wise counsel.

Using This Anecdote

This story can be used in a variety of ways. It can be used on a personal level to motivate individuals to set their goals high. Or, more broadly, it can be used to set goals high on a company level as well. In either case, always having something to shoot for is critical. It gives life purpose. Try this: "I see no reason why we shouldn't set our goals higher, why we shouldn't strive even harder and not settle for the merely attainable when we can go for a much bigger prize. I'm reminded of a story Ted Turner told about advice he got from his dad, who thought he had achieved everything he wanted in life . . ."

Source
Ted Turner, *Call Me Ted* (New York: Grand Central Publishing, 2008), p. 56.

Ted Turner

TURNER ENTERPRISES

Credit on the Barrel

> Financing a New Venture
> Risk Taking
> Striking Even When Weak

Good thing he'd always been a smooth talker. Ted Turner's story of obtaining financing to get his signature CNN network off the ground sounds like a business potboiler. Sure, he had assets, but not enough to see a company that size and with that kind of ambition all the way through to profitability. He faced two options: Either sell more assets or take on more debt. Access to capital was not as easy as it looked. His ventures had previously been considered risky. Turner had already sold his radio and billboard business and was not ready to give up either of his premier sports assets. The Atlanta Braves and the Hawks were off the table. He was, however, ready to sell one of his biggest assets, WRET-TV, in Charlotte, North Carolina, which he had bought for $1 million eight years earlier. It was now worth $20 million. Not the most strategic asset in his portfolio, the station was eventually sold to Westinghouse. That money would help, but it was nowhere near enough to keep CNN running.

Then the WRET-TV sale hit a snag. Another major problem arose getting time on a satellite so CNN could even work. It took herculean effort, but both problems would eventually be resolved so the fledgling network could get off the ground. Throughout it all, though, Turner pursued a strategy of using his weakness to his advantage. He says that he pursued a course similar to that of the German general Irwin Rommel, widely known as the Desert Fox. For example, with his forces low on fuel, Rommel would roll the dice and attack the Allies when they *least* expected it, quickly over-run them, then capture their fuel depots so he could continue his offensive. Turner saw his financing of CNN in similar terms. If only he could get enough money to just make it through the first year, he could then prove CNN's concept was viable and access to capital would become easier in a virtuous circle. And even if they ran out of money, they still would have created something valuable enough to sell. Fortunately, he never needed to. His strategy paid off—and then some.

Using This Anecdote

Even the most successful ventures were often huge risks in the beginning, with lots of doubters, particularly among bankers. Finding a way around the dilemma of getting financing for a good idea, when you don't have the track record to prove creditworthiness, has vexed many an entrepreneur. Turner's story illustrates the importance of believing in the soundness of your concept and doing everything you can to get to the starting gate. Once you're there, your success in proving the concept can create a bandwagon effect that gets around the dilemma and gets the credit flowing. Try this: "All ventures must take risks. Even some of the biggest names out there started out as little more than a good idea and a mad dash to get capital . . ."

Source

Ted Turner, *Call Me Ted* (New York: Grand Central Publishing, 2008), pp. 183–189.

TURNER ENTERPRISES

Clean Out Your Desk

> Firing People
> Cleaning House

Sometimes a little housecleaning can make a huge difference. Early in Ted Turner's career, in the late 1960s, he already had five radio stations in his portfolio, but none in his hometown of Atlanta. Turner was soon looking for a media property closer to home. Turner tells the story of how an opportunity opened up when he saw an ad for a UHF television station that had been advertising on one of his billboards. The station, WJRJ, had gone public but was hemorrhaging money badly. Turner, who had never owned a TV station up to that point, sensed an opportunity. He did not have enough money to go forward with an outright sale. Instead, a stock swap was negotiated making Turner the largest shareholder in the combined company. After a drawn-out FCC approval process, the deal was finalized and the WJRJ call letters were changed over to WTCG, for Turner Communications Group.

But when Turner went to see the station he had just bought, he was appalled. It was one of the worst-run operations he had ever encountered in all his years in business. He says that most of the thirty-five people he had inherited were "either lazy, on drugs, or both." The lackadaisical attitude started at the top. He tells the story of walking into the general manager's office, only to find him with his feet up on the desk, reading the *Wall Street Journal*. He scolded him, saying he should be out aggressively selling advertising instead of reading the paper. Turner soon invested in new people and new equipment to turn the operation around. After one year, of the thirty-five original employees he had inherited, only two were left: the receptionist and the janitor. The rest were gone—forever. They had stood in the way of the progress Turner wanted. Two years later, after much effort, the station broke even. A year after that, it was generating more than $1 million in profits. Sometimes you have to change almost the entire team to start winning games again.

Using This Anecdote

Serious underperformers can sometimes stand in the way of ambitious plans ever coming to fruition. In these circumstances, marginal changes won't cut it. Hard as these decisions are, sometimes they have to be made. Try this: "No one likes cutbacks, but every business goes through it. For example, Ted Turner would likely not be where he is today if he hadn't made some tough choices in letting people go . . ."

Source
Ted Turner, *Call Me Ted* (New York: Grand Central Publishing, 2008), pp. 91–94, 105.

> Selling Advertising
> Demographics
> Sales

When you've got lemons, the best strategy—always—is to make lemonade. Media mogul Ted Turner's second foray into television was with a bankrupt UHF station in Charlotte, North Carolina. He had bought it for $1 million of his own money, renaming it after his own initials, WRET (Robert Edward Turner). The station was seriously undercapitalized and not bringing in enough money to stay afloat. In addition to telethons—which Turner jokingly calls "beg-a-thons"—he tells the story of how he poured much of his energy into bringing in new advertising revenue. Going out on a lot of these sales calls himself, Turner says selling advertising on WRET was anything but an easy sell. UHF stations were hardly where the action was even back then. They were often difficult to find on one's television, while VHF stations were readily accessible. Undeterred, Turner had ready answers for all these objections.

Because WRET included programming in the 1970s such as *The*

Andy Griffith Show, which was shot in black-and-white, some advertisers were skeptical. They said the station was behind the times, especially with more people wanting programming in color. Turner would fire back saying his black-and-white programming only meant that their commercials—shot in color—would stand out in contrast that much more! Advertisers also said his programming was too old-fashioned. His viewers were neither a young nor sophisticated enough demographic for their needs. Turner would tell them they had it all wrong. "Our viewers," he says, "were actually much smarter than our competitors' because you had to be a genius to figure out how to pull down a UHF signal!" Persistence personified!

Using This Anecdote

One should always be ready to make a silk purse out of a sow's ear when necessary. Turner needed to turn an argument against into an argument for, and he was clearly prepared. Try this: "Sometimes we don't have the luxury of playing a winning hand, but we still have to play the cards we're dealt. That reminds me of a story Ted Turner tells about his early career in television, where creativity and persistence were needed to stay afloat . . ."

Source
Ted Turner, *Call Me Ted* (New York: Grand Central Publishing, 2008), pp. 97–98.

Sam Walton

WALMART

Out of Thin Air

> Bureaucracy
> Containing Costs
> Expenses
> Slim Margins

Walmart founder Sam Walton tells the story of his desire to see his company control costs even as the original store he founded was growing into the largest retailer in the United States. One of his biggest fears was that as his company grew, he did not want to see Walmart become a huge bureaucracy. He says he always tried to operate his stores on 2 percent of sales, meaning that 2 percent of the store's sales would be enough to keep the store afloat, paying for salaries, information technology, and other expenses.

Years later, after he had already achieved great success, he tells the story of how he was repeatedly asked how he came up with the 2 percent formula when most of his competitors were operating at 5 percent margins. His answer? "The truth is, I just pulled it out of the air." He had always operated his stores in a lean manner anyhow, and the 2 percent figure fit. Add that to the fact that they operated with fewer people and did not spend much on fancy executive offices, and the lower figure makes a lot of sense. If anything, that figure reflected a gut instinct already following a winning formula. Although his company's corporate offices would never win any decorating awards, that was just fine with Walton. "Just ask our shareholders," he says.

Using This Anecdote

Containing costs should be a part of everyday business. Try this: "Curbing costs should be considered a part of the way we think and work here. Sam Walton, the founder of Walmart, had made this so much a part of his thinking that he was already operating 3 percent below the industry average when it came to running his stores. He pulled that figure out of thin air, and it still proved to be the right way forward . . ."

Source

Sam Walton, *Sam Walton: Made in America, My Story* (New York: Doubleday, 1992), pp. 230–231.

Sam Walton

WALMART

"Jelly Doughnut?"

> Distribution
> "Early to Bed, Early to Rise . . ."
> Gathering Info

Sam Walton clearly was an early riser. He was also very clever when it came to getting objective information. One of Walmart's secrets in standing above other retailers was the fact they had their own distribution centers as well as a private trucking fleet. This was something that was not widely the case among the stores' competitors. Advantages included shorter lead times, more reliability, as well as the ability to find even more efficiencies in-house, in the end maximizing Walmart's in-stock position. Simply put, product was there when the customer was there. Walton says that Walmart may have one of the country's largest private trucking fleets, with their own loyal drivers. He says they're not just driving trucks from point to point but are actual Walmart employees committed to servicing the stores they deliver to. It is more than just hauling some other company's products to stores, making the delivery, and then driving back to get more.

These truck drivers are also eyes and ears for how Walmart stores in different locations are doing.

Walton tells the story of how he would often show up in the truckers' break room at four in the morning, armed with doughnuts and lots of questions before they headed out on the road again. Walton would spend hours grilling the drivers on how the stores they delivered to were doing. He would ask pointed questions like how many shoppers they saw, what improvements were being made or not being made, how people acted when shopping there, what merchandise was moving, etc. This helped Walton get better and probably more objective information on stores than if he had visited them on his own, something that logistically would have not been in the cards.

Using This Anecdote

Walmart's decision to go it alone in distribution gave them many benefits, including allowing management to keep an eye on how their stores were doing. A management secret weapon, if you will. Try this: "Good intelligence on the business is key to figuring out how we're *really* doing. Of course, we need the raw numbers, but sometimes the most interesting information comes from what you see with your own eyes. That reminds me of a story Sam Walton told in his autobiography about leveraging an idea that already helped his company stand out . . ."

Source
Sam Walton, *Sam Walton: Made in America, My Story* (New York: Doubleday, 1992), pp. 210–211.

Sam Walton

WALMART

Know Thyself

> Delegating
> Different Skill Sets
> Hiring Talent
> Management Team

You can't do everything perfectly. Nor should you even try. One of the key functions of management is finding talented individuals and letting them do what they do best. Regarding an incident in which a number of Walmart executives ended up leaving the company, Sam Walton says that this may have been a huge blessing in disguise since it allowed him the opportunity to hire David Glass, an executive whom he had been trying to woo for some time. In looking back at the company's rise, Walton writes that one of the secrets of Walmart's success was that instead of looking for clones of himself, he put together a strong management team with talents he personally did not possess.

He tells the story of his team consisting over time of one old-school, get-it-done executive; one methodical organizer; one computer whiz; one shoot-from-the hip exec with a store manager's attitude;

and one who was always calm, cool, and collected in a crisis. Each brought something different to the table and had his or her own role to play. More importantly, each complemented the others. "From day one," writes Walton, "we just always found the folks who had the qualities that neither [my brother] Bud nor I had. And they fit into the niches as the company grew." It takes a lot of self-awareness to know what to look for, but good managers can do it.

Using This Anecdote

A key function of management is not necessarily control, but allowing freedom for talented individuals to make their contribution to the team based on what they do best and what they're passionate about. Try this: "Managers with too much pride and ego don't always make it. They need instead to fill in the gaps where they themselves are sometimes weak. One of the key functions of a good manager is to find people who have skills they don't necessarily have and let them shine at what they're passionate about and do best . . ."

Source
Sam Walton, *Sam Walton: Made in America, My Story* (New York: Doubleday, 1992), p. 154.

Sam Walton

WALMART

"Can You Spot Me Twenty Bucks?"

> Borrowing Money
> Cheapness
> Frugality
> Watching Expenses

His prices were cheap and, well . . . so was he. Sam Walton was renowned for his frugality, a trait that he instilled throughout Walmart, making it part of the company's DNA. David Glass, a former Walmart CEO, tells the story of a business trip he once took with the boss. He writes that unless he read the company's proxy statement every year, he would have thought Walton was always flat broke. During a trip from New York City to Dayton, Ohio, Walton told Glass that he had no money on him and asked if he could borrow some. Glass looked in his wallet and handed him two twenties. Walton then told Glass, "I won't need both of these, let me borrow *one*."

Walton himself admitted to being frugal, saying that on such trips he and his executives would often sleep two to a room to save money. They ate at a lot of relatively inexpensive family restaurants and stayed at discount chain hotels. One early store manager even mentioned that on a buying trip in Chicago, they stayed eight in a room to save money! The rationale behind all this frugality? Understanding the value of a buck. Walton writes: "A lot of what goes on these days with high-flying companies and these overpaid CEOs who're really just looting from the top and aren't watching out for anybody but themselves really upsets me." It's one of the things wrong with American business these days, he concludes.

Using This Anecdote

While the Walmart example may seem a bit extreme for most companies, it makes an important point. At the end of the day, if you can honestly say in front of the owners of the company—the shareholders—that your expenses are justified, then you're fine. If not, then maybe it's time to think about company spending habits. Try this: "We need to keep expenses under control. While this may be an extreme example in business history, I think the story of Walmart illustrates an attitude we need more of these days at our own company . . ."

Source
Sam Walton, *Sam Walton: Made in America, My Story* (New York: Doubleday, 1992), pp. 9–10.

Sam Walton

WALMART

Caught Red-Handed

> Competitive Research
> Embarrassing Incidents
> Forgiveness
> Honesty
> Getting Caught

Not everyone would admit to a story like this. Sam Walton tells of one time when he was conducting "on-site research" in San Diego. He was scoping out one of his competitors, walking around the aisles with a small tape recorder. He used the small device to record prices as well as his impressions of the store for later use. As he was walking down one aisle, Walton was approached by an employee who told him point-blank that he was violating store policy. He asked Walton to surrender his tape recorder. They would need to erase everything on it. Walton knew he was caught red-handed, especially since he had the same policy at his own stores! He was happy to oblige, except for one thing. On that same tape, he also had information he had recorded on different stores, and he wasn't ready to erase that part of the recording just yet.

He then told the employee that he'd be happy to turn the tape over to him, but he needed to write a personal note to the owner of the store, whom he knew. In the note, he admitted to taking notes but asked if he could still get the tape back. It was perfectly fine if the owner erased the material dealing with that particular store. But could he leave the parts dealing with the other stores unerased? Walton then handed both the tape and the note over to the employee, probably expecting to get nothing back other than a sternly worded message. About four days later, to his surprise, he got a nice letter from his competitor with the tape enclosed. Nothing was erased. "He probably treated me better than I deserved," Walton says. Not every example of getting caught doing opposition research ends like this, but it certainly does speak to forgiveness.

Using This Anecdote

This humorous story can be used when describing doing research on your competitor, although *not* urging employees to break any rules, however! Of course, this example is from an age well before the Internet, which makes prices more transparent, but it's amusing nonetheless. Try this: "We need to find out more about what our competitor is up to, what it is that they're doing that's giving them so much success. But play fair. I'm reminded of a story from Sam Walton when he was doing some research on a competitor himself but got caught . . ."

Source
Sam Walton, *Sam Walton: Made in America, My Story* (New York: Doubleday, 1992), p. 202.

Sam Walton

WALMART

"Give Me a 'W'! Give Me an 'A'!"

> Brand Name
> Naming a Company
> Saving Money
> Simplicity

Simplicity helps—plus, it saves on signage. One of Walmart's first managers, Bob Bogle, tells the story of how the company's name was chosen. It was 1962. He and Walton were flying over the mountains of northern Arkansas in a private plane. Walton pulled out a piece of paper from his pocket and handed it to Bogle. On it, Walton had scribbled a few suggested names for the retail company they were about to launch. All of them were on the long side. Many consisting of three or four words. None would do.

Bogle thought it over, turned to Walton, and said that his Scottish roots made it hard for him to accept longer names that would cost too much to illuminate on storefronts. "I'd just keep the Walton name and make it a place to shop," Bogle said. He then wrote out: "W-A-L-M-A-R-T." It was short—just seven letters. And it would save on signage. Not to mention, it neatly abbreviated the company founder's name and said what the business was about. Walton didn't say anything the rest of the plane trip, and the subject was dropped. A few days later, Bogle was at the first store they were setting up when he saw that their sign maker had already put up "W A L." The sign man was on a ladder just about to put up an "M." "You don't have to be a genius to figure out what the name was going to be," he says. Indeed. Nor would it be the last sign they put up, either.

Using This Anecdote

The thinking behind naming a company, or naming a business project or initiative for that matter, is: simplicity, simplicity, simplicity. Try this: "We need to come up with a good name for this new (business, project). I don't know what it is yet, but I'm reminded of a story I read about how they came up with the name for Walmart . . ."

Source
Sam Walton, *Sam Walton: Made in America, My Story* (New York: Doubleday, 1992), p. 44.

Sam Walton

WALMART

The Times They Are A-Changin'

> Being Ahead of the Curve
> Discounting
> Riding a Wave
> Risk Taking

Stand still long enough and the market will pass you by. By the early 1960s, long before he had founded his first Walmart, Sam Walton had started noticing the writing on the wall for the retailing industry at the time. Larger discount stores were beginning to take root, operating with profit margins previously unheard of. Walton tells the story of spending time studying the phenomenon, visiting many of these new stores across the country, including one in a nearby town whose founder's philosophy probably best summed up the new approach: "Buy it low, stack it high, and sell it cheap."

Although it was still a small segment of the market at that time, Walton was convinced that the high margins meant that large discount stores were the wave of the future. He faced a choice: Either join the bandwagon now and be a player, or get swallowed up by others later. Walton decided to catch the wave rather than be swamped by it. He, his wife, and his business partners had to pledge their houses and all their property to allow them to borrow what they needed to get started. It was a huge risk since they were already heavily leveraged. If the enterprise had failed, they would have gone bankrupt. Still, the formula worked, and the company went on to enormous success. But in those early days, it was never a guarantee.

Using This Anecdote

Some of the biggest success stories in business follow a similar pattern: Watch trends carefully; decide whether to join them, ignore them, or go your own way; then place your bet. In Walton's case, that bet paid off handsomely. Try this: "You may not believe this, but the biggest retailer in this country started off by putting his own house and property down as collateral. That's how Sam Walton started when he saw which way retailing was headed. As we look to invest in new markets, we don't have to take quite the level of risk Walton took, but if he could do that with his own money, we should have the same vision and commitment . . ."

Source
Sam Walton, *Sam Walton: Made in America, My Story* (New York: Doubleday, 1992), pp. 8–9.

Sam Walton

WALMART

The Saturday Morning Meeting

> Building Team Spirit
> Celebrities
> Creative Meetings
> Reviewing Results
> "Turnabout's Fair Play"

Don't forget to set your alarm Friday night. One of Walmart founder's Sam Walton's legendary management techniques was conducting Saturday meetings where a variety of topics were discussed, including best-practice sharing, the latest management techniques from competitors, as well as business literature. Nonexecutives would be invited as well. Speakers included outside guests, Walmart associates who came up with money-saving ideas, and others. The Saturday meetings would mix business with pleasure, the serious with the silly, pointing out company success stories and praising those involved, while also pointing out the company's weaknesses. They were also, in Walton's own words, "managed fun" to rally the troops. Sometimes there would be singing, other times group calisthenics, and so on.

Guests would range from the head of a small company with an

innovative idea to CEO legends like Jack Welch. One Saturday meeting even featured a mock boxing match between Walton and Olympic boxing gold medal–winner Sugar Ray Leonard. One executive tells the story of how Walton had announced at one Saturday meeting that in three weeks this particular individual would be singing "Red River Valley" in front of the entire group, even though Walton knew full well that the guy had a terrible singing voice and could never possibly carry a tune. He had only wanted to serve this individual a helping of humble pie for something he had done. But the exec turned the tables on Walton . . . He secretly organized a group of others with stronger voices than his. On the appointed Saturday, the chorus ended up drowning out his voice as he gamely sang along. The ruse worked, all in good fun.

Using This Anecdote

Dedication is important in any company (after all, not everybody was initially thrilled about surrendering their Saturday mornings), but when making sacrifices, poking fun at one's self and lightening the mood can build team spirit. Try this: "There's a time to be serious about the business, but there's no reason we can't also learn and grow in a way that's spontaneous and fun. Sam Walton, the founder of Walmart, proved that at his legendary Saturday meetings with company executives. At one of them . . ."

Source
Sam Walton, *Sam Walton: Made in America, My Story* (New York: Doubleday, 1992), pp. 164–166.

> Sticking to Your Principles
> Creative Ideas
> Store Greeters

It wasn't originally an idea from headquarters. Walmart didn't *always* have the store greeters they're widely known for. Walton tells the story of how he and another Walmart executive first encountered a greeter at one of their stores in Crowley, Louisiana, in 1980. As the pair entered the building, they were greeted by an older gentleman who cheerily welcomed them, saying he'd be happy to answer any questions they had about the store. Walton was floored. Once the associate got over the shock of meeting the chairman, they spent a few minutes talking. Walton and the other executive soon learned that this particular store had apparently been having problems with shoplifting and the manager wanted to make sure his inventory wasn't being stolen. He didn't want to post someone at the entrance solely as a guard against shoplifters. He correctly assumed that might intimidate customers—especially the vast majority who were honest. At the same time, though, with a small number of customers sneaking out the door with stolen merchandise, he needed to send a strong—but friendly—signal that *someone* was watching the store.

Walton loved this practical approach. It balanced being customer-friendly with watching the bottom line. He brought the idea back to the headquarters in Bentonville, Arkansas. But it met stiff resistance. Many saw it as a waste of money and time, but Walton was, in the words of one executive, "relentless" on this issue. He thought all Walmart stores should have greeters. Despite the opposition, Sam pushed and pushed and it finally went through. His vindication, he says, came when he entered a Kmart in Illinois in 1989 and found that they had posted greeters at their front door. Imitation can often be the sincerest form of flattery—or at least a sign you're on the right path.

Using This Anecdote

Sometimes when you believe strongly enough in what you see as a good idea, you have to keep pushing, especially if you have a creative solution to a serious problem such as shoplifting. Try this: "Sometimes the best solutions are the simplest and the ones that play to human psychology. You've all probably been in a Walmart and have likely seen those store greeters, right? What you may not know is what the motivation behind that concept was. It was actually a very clever solution to a serious problem . . ."

Source
Sam Walton, *Sam Walton: Made in America, My Story* (New York: Doubleday, 1992), pp. 229–230.

Jack Welch

GENERAL ELECTRIC

Permission to Speak

> Empowering Employees
> Process Improvement
> Bottom-Up Thinking
> Permission to Talk

The most useful ideas don't always come from the top of the org chart. They can arise from anywhere in the organization. During his tenure as General Electric's CEO, business legend Jack Welch says he was determined to turn GE into a learning organization, breaking down hierarchical boundaries. Based on the great success of his Crotonville management training center, he moved quickly to spread this method throughout the entire company in a program called "Work Out." Not exactly physical fitness, "Work Out" actually meant taking unneeded work out of processes by bringing managers and employees together to discuss challenges and examine options under the eye of a neutral facilitator. Welch tells the story of one Work Out he attended in GE's appliance business.

Along with more than two dozen employees sitting in a Holiday Inn in Lexington, Kentucky, Welch watched as an employee gave a presentation on how to improve refrigerator door manufacturing. Just as he was describing a process on one part along the assembly line, the plant's chief steward got frustrated, stood up, and interrupted the presentation. He grabbed a marker and proceeded to tell everyone how the assembly line really worked, based on his own direct experience. He then sketched out in detail how the process could be improved. Impressed, the group quickly accepted his solution. There was no way senior management could have come up with such a detailed solution. They weren't close enough to the business. The key? Giving permission for people to truly speak their minds and tapping into the hands-on knowledge of those actually doing the job. Welch adds that another worker later told him something similar: "For twenty-five years, you've paid for my hands when you could have had my brain as well—for nothing."

Using This Anecdote

Too often, people are intimidated by those above them with bigger salaries and more impressive titles. The fact is, the right answers don't always come from the top. They can come from anywhere within the company. But people sometimes need permission to speak up. You can start by saying, "I know the answer to this challenge is out there, somewhere in this room perhaps. Before I go any further, though, I want to share with you a story I heard from GE that I think speaks exactly to what I want you to see here today—namely, that the answers may not come from where you think . . ."

Source
Jack Welch, *Straight from the Gut* (New York: Warner Business Books, 2001), pp. 182–184.

Jack Welch

GENERAL ELECTRIC

Ka-Boom!

> Permission to Fail
> "Pushing the Envelope"
> Risk Taking
> Forgiving Mistakes

Early in Jack Welch's career at GE, he blew the roof off the company—literally. Only twenty-eight years old and in his third year there, Welch was put in charge of a project that involved experimenting with a chemical process. Sitting at his desk one day, he heard a tremendous explosion coming from the company's pilot plant across the street. Part of the roof had been blown off and debris was flying everywhere. Welch raced as quickly as he could to the scene. He soon arrived to find that—fortunately—no one had been injured. The safety features had functioned as intended and the explosion was directed upward. The damage was done, though. Not just to the building, but potentially to Welch's career since he was the line manager in charge.

The next day, Welch had to explain the whole incident to his boss's boss. While GE managers are expected to develop new ideas for products and push the envelope, blowing up facilities didn't exactly figure into those expectations. Nervous and uncertain whether his career was finished, Welch sat down and explained the situation in detail. He lucked out. The individual he met with had a PhD in chemical engineering from MIT, so he understood the scientific experimentation that had led to the explosion. He questioned Welch almost like a professor, before eventually saying, "It's better we learned about this problem now rather than later when we had a large-scale operation going. Thank God no one was hurt." Welch says that this individual's reaction truly impressed him. "When people make mistakes, the last thing they need is discipline. It's time for encouragement and confidence building." In other words, they need permission to fail, to learn from mistakes, and to move on. Without it, people are only likely to play it safe—with limited progress as a result.

Using This Anecdote

Think about what would have happened if Welch had gotten fired. The company's history would have likely been very different. Encourage people to push the envelope. As long as they understand why they failed and work to correct mistakes, risk taking can be a very positive mind-set for your company. It's how you stay on the cutting edge. Try this: "I'd like to see more risk taking here. While I don't encourage you to do exactly what Jack Welch did early in his career, it's an interesting story that speaks to a corporate culture that encourages people to go for it and doesn't penalize them if they fail . . ."

Source
Jack Welch, *Straight from the Gut* (New York: Warner Business Books, 2001), pp. 27–29.

Jack Welch

GENERAL ELECTRIC

Window or Aisle?

> Assembling Management Teams
> Hypothetical Situations
> Succession Planning

Great CEOs are always thinking about the future—and that includes anticipation of what will happen when they're not in the picture anymore. Jack Welch tells the story of how he was chosen to succeed Reg Jones, GE's legendary chairman and Welch's predecessor. In early 1979, media speculation was circulating about who would be the next chairman once Jones headed off to retirement. Welch tells the story of being called into Jones's office and asked to shut the door. Jones then asked Welch a hypothetical question that he prefaced by supposing that the two of them were flying in a company plane. Suppose the plane crashed and both were killed. Who, Jones asked, should be the next chairman of GE? Welch then tried to argue that he actually survived the crash and should be the next head. Jones shot back saying no dice: They're both gone, someone else has to take the helm. Welch, now accepting the rules of the game, then went through a list of con-

tenders, ranking them according to their relative strengths and weaknesses.

Welch says that Jones was using the so-called airplane interview to
figure out who could work with whom. (The same interviews had
apparently been conducted with other contenders.) About six months
later, Jones calls Welch into the office again and asked a variation of
his previous question. This time, however, Jones didn't survive—but
Welch did. Without hesitation, Welch said he should be the successor.
Jones then quizzed him on whom he would put on his management
team and what the top issues were that he would address as chair.
Turns out that, to gauge where everyone ranked, he did the exact
same thing with a number of other candidates, and played it poker-
faced right to the end.

Using This Anecdote

This is a great story for talking either about succession planning or the
chemistry needed to put together winning management teams. Try
this: "As you put your teams together, remember that chemistry is
really important. There's an amusing story in Jack Welch's autobiography of how his predecessor teased out information on whom Welch
would be comfortable working with in setting up his own management team . . ."

Source
Jack Welch, *Straight from the Gut* (New York: Warner Business Books,
2001), pp. 78–80.

Jack Welch

GENERAL ELECTRIC

Some of You Won't Be Here Next Year . . .

> Fitting In
> Living the Culture
> Letting People Go

Great results, but are you really on board? At GE's 1992 annual operating managers' meeting in Boca Raton, Florida, Jack Welch spoke of creating a "boundary-less" culture at GE. They would encourage people to work collaboratively, putting teams ahead of individual ego, to seek out best practices from other companies and to knock down as many walls as possible throughout the business. He said there were four types of managers at GE. The first type delivered on his or her commitments and shared the company's values. Theirs would be an easy call to make—their futures were ensured. The second type didn't meet commitments and didn't share the values. That call was also easy. Unpleasant, but easy—*they're out.* The third type missed their targets but shared all the values. This group was usually given second or third chances, where comebacks are always possible. The fourth group was the most difficult of all, however. They made all their numbers and hit their targets, *but* they didn't share the values. All too often, they were autocratic managers. They'd often get results by bullying instead of inspiring those who worked for them.

Welch, in describing the "boundary-less" culture he wanted to see throughout the company, told the group that GE could not afford to keep Type Four managers. He mentioned that four corporate officers—without naming them publicly—had been asked to leave the company after fitting into that category. He described how one manager had never embraced the Work Out concept, another couldn't build a strong team, and still another never really bought into globalization. The audience sat stunned. They had been accustomed to the usual "he or she left to 'pursue other interests'" boilerplate, but this was a level of candor they were not used to hearing. "You could hear a pin drop," Welch says. "When I used the lack of boundary-less behavior as one of the principal reasons for a manager leaving, the idea really hit home. You could feel the audience thinking, this is for real. They mean it."

Using This Anecdote

Strong corporate cultures, with people getting on board and not just talking the talk but also walking the walk, are needed at every company. The fact that GE let go of people because they didn't make their numbers is hardly worthy of a headline. The fact that they let people go who did perform but didn't *believe*, that's something very different. Try this: "We need each of you to buy into this company's values; otherwise we're all going in different directions. I'm reminded of a story Jack Welch told in his autobiography where he talked about what he saw as the four types of managers and how even performers have to be let go . . ."

Source
Jack Welch, *Straight from the Gut* (New York: Warner Business Books, 2001), pp. 188–189.

Jack Welch

GENERAL ELECTRIC

"The Envelope Please!"

> The Fog of War
> Strategic Planning
> Making Adjustments to Fit Real-World Circumstances
> Risk

Overplan—and you'll likely underachieve. In a speech he delivered early in his tenure as CEO, Jack Welch told an audience of financial services representatives in New York that he wished he could pull a sealed envelope from his jacket pocket containing GE's grand strategy for the decade ahead—and voilà—all their questions would be answered. He said it couldn't be done. He then quoted from a letter to *Fortune* magazine originally written by a planning manager from Bendix. Welch said that it was difficult to improve on what this manager said. Citing the book *On War* by military theorist Carl von Clausewitz, the letter said that despite the best of intentions, strategic planning cannot be reduced to a simple formula that must be blindly followed like some kind of paint-by-numbers exercise. In business, just as in the fog of war, there will always be chance events. Plans gone awry. You never really know for sure what your opponent will do to counter your moves. In that kind of uncertain environment, what counts more are human factors: leadership, morale, and instincts.

The letter mentioned that the Prussian general staff never expected a plan of operations to survive beyond the first contact with the enemy. "Strategy was not a lengthy action plan," the Bendix manager concluded, saying that Clausewitz advocated the "evolution of a central idea through continually changing circumstances." While business and war obviously have very different objectives, a cookbook approach to any challenge will never work in the unfolding situations of the real world. The fog of war—like the fog of business—makes it impossible to plan for everything. But having the right people in place with the right skills and the right instincts to adapt to changing circumstances greatly increases the chances of success.

Using This Anecdote

Even the best-laid plans can—and often do—fall woefully short when they run up against reality. You may have the best plan in the world, but do you really know what your competition will do in response? What if new laws are passed affecting your business? What if there's a product defect no one saw coming? What counts more is having a solid overall strategy and then putting people in place who can adapt nimbly, quickly, and intelligently to circumstances that will inevitably change. Try this: "Try as we might, we cannot plan for everything. We cannot control the field completely, no company can. I'm reminded of a speech Jack Welch gave where he said he could not create a grand strategy for GE . . ."

Source
Jack Welch, *Straight from the Gut* (New York: Warner Business Books, 2001), pp. 447–448.

Meg Whitman

EBAY

Let Your Conscience Be Your Guide

> Doing the Right Thing
> Contracts
> Customer Loyalty
> Technical Failures

Never let a good crisis go to waste. And this was one heck of a crisis. Former eBay CEO Meg Whitman tells the story of how early in the company's history it was faced with one of its worst nightmare situations to date: a twenty-two-hour system outage that nearly sank the fledgling business. The site ground to a halt. Customers could neither buy nor sell. And the media smelled blood in the water. Would the company survive? Or would it follow the path of so many other online companies onto the ash heap of business history? CNN was trying to get gotcha video of the company responding to the crisis. One commentator said the situation was as if all Sears stores around the country had closed simultaneously and they could not say when they were going to open up again.

While the technical issues were finally solved and the system eventually went back online, the crisis was far from over. Whitman tells the story of how she entered a conference room where bleary-eyed employees were discussing the company's service agreement with sellers. The fine print said that they owed money only to those sellers whose auctions ended during any outage. The problem was all auctions—including those that ended later—were affected. They calculated that the difference between honoring the agreement to the letter and compensating all losses at about $5 million. No small amount. If paid, it would mean missing quarterly earnings projections. Whitman listened to the conversation and then asked the group: "What's the right thing to do here?" She then left the room. The conversation ended right there. They would refund everyone. The company's CFO later said, "People always know the right thing to do, but sometimes they need the leadership to remind them." After the company explained the rationale behind the decision, Wall Street did not abandon eBay for not making their numbers—nor did customers abandon them for doing the right thing, either.

Using This Anecdote

Sometimes in business, being penny-wise and pound-foolish is not the way to go. Yes, contracts say such-and-such obligation must be met, but there's nothing to stop you from going beyond the letter of the agreement and doing the right thing. In fact, by doing so, you may get more benefit over the long term than you could potentially lose over the short term. Try this: "I know this is a tough decision, and yes, we should honor our agreements, but we're facing more than just a question of a single contract. I'm reminded of the story Meg Whitman tells of eBay's early history . . ."

Source
Meg Whitman, *The Power of Many* (New York: Crown Publishers, 2010), pp. 1–3.

Meg Whitman

EBAY

Shooting for the Moon

> Stretch Goals
> Dot-coms
> Moving Beyond One's Comfort Zone
> Risks

She knew the risks and rolled the dice. It was September 2000 and the dot-com world was crashing. As the bubble was bursting, talk went from dot-com hype to dot-bomb reality, and the public's and investors' confidence in online businesses was plummeting. Former eBay CEO Meg Whitman tells the story of how she was hosting an annual Analyst Day where they would present plans for the coming year. Despite their dot-com brethren dropping like flies, eBay was still doing well. Companies were being acquired and integrated, revenues and profits were up. In fact, as eBay's management team was preparing for the meeting, they needed a rallying cry—something that would bring the message together and give the company a stretch goal to strive for.

Usually, these meetings involve upbeat CEOs talking about future prospects, growth opportunities, saying optimistic but intentionally vague phrases like "the sky's the limit," etc. The one thing you're not likely to hear, however, are hard numbers. In discussing what the rallying cry should be, Whitman tells the story of how she and others decided on a risky move. They were going to put a number out there. So, standing before a group of analysts—BlackBerrys at the ready— she announced that eBay's revenues would go from $430 million in 2000 to $3 billion by 2005. The audience was stunned. Typing furiously, they started sending out alerts. A friend and financial analyst later confided to Whitman that that was perhaps one of the most unwise things she had ever seen a CEO do. Committing to a number was not only a risk for Whitman personally, it was a risk for the company overall. Whitman stuck to her guns, though. The company now had a major goal to rally behind. By 2005, it turns out, eBay indeed did not achieve $3 billion in revenues. It hit $4.5 billion instead. "Stretch goals are an important part of leadership," Whitman says. "To do significant things, things that are important and worth doing, sometimes leaders need to take a deep breath and jump."

Using This Anecdote

Did Whitman take a risk in saying revenues would multiple fivefold in five years? Absolutely. But she was confident enough in the business and knew her employees needed a stretch goal to keep their motivation level high. Try this: "I know we're going out on a limb here, but it's been done before by others equally confident in their business model. I'm reminded of when Meg Whitman . . ."

Source
Meg Whitman, *The Power of Many* (New York: Crown Publishers, 2010), pp. 225–229.

Meg Whitman

EBAY

Online Power

> Accountability
> Listening to the Customer
> The Power of Many

If it ain't broke, don't fix it. Former eBay CEO Meg Whitman says the need to listen and be accountable to customers in a transparent organization is critical. She tells the story of a relatively new employee who had been tasked with revamping eBay's rating system. Instead of the single star to indicate who had achieved a satisfaction rating, this person proposed a system involving a variety of color-coded stars showing how many positive reviews an individual had received for transactions. The highest level would be the image of a shooting star, and so on. The new system was then launched online.

As Whitman tells the story, it took only a few minutes before feedback flooded in. And it kept coming. And coming. Some challenged why eBay was changing the rating system in the first place. Others had more petty concerns, such as not liking the particular shade of one or another color. Others questioned her right to change anything at all without consulting eBay users first. Pretty soon, the volume of emails increased to the point where the person who made the changes was spending three hours each day just answering queries on the new system alone. Finally, this individual met with a top exec and a solution was found. Apologize for the change, ask for users' ideas, and redo the system. It was a raw lesson for a company that prided itself on the "power of many," but in this case had gone with the instinct of the few. Since people using eBay were relying on the company to make money, and the Internet enabled group collaboration anyhow, the need for users to be part of the decision-making process was an important one.

Using This Anecdote

Not all decisions can be made by fiat. The old command-and-control model of yore may have worked well years ago. But in the digital age—and especially with online-based companies—you really do have to rely more on the wisdom of the group. Try this: "Let's not lose sight of the fact that we can no longer really impose decisions from above and expect customers to accept everything uncritically. It doesn't always work that way. I'm reminded of a story Meg Whitman tells about eBay . . ."

Source
Meg Whitman, *The Power of Many* (New York: Crown Publishers, 2010), pp. 145–146.

> Culture Clash
> Mergers and Acquisitions
> Pruning
> Portfolio

Sometimes success can breed overconfidence. Former eBay CEO Meg Whitman tells a story of when the company's stock had topped $200 a share in 1999 and they were looking for acquisitions that would help them build their collectible business and migrate the brand toward higher-priced items. One company in particular caught their attention: Butterfield & Butterfield, a venerable auction company that was in the same league with equally renowned names like Sotheby's and Christie's. This San Francisco–based auction house had impeccable credentials, a highly trained staff of experts, and a white-gloved clientele. By bringing the company into the fold, Whitman hoped to attract higher-end buyers and sellers to eBay while also expanding Butterfield's market reach online.

The company paid $260 million for Butterfield and Wall Street applauded the deal. During the negotiations, however, Whitman had already seen early signs of a potential culture clash. Most Butterfield & Butterfield employees were at least twenty years older than the average eBay employee. The offices were decked out in mahogany furniture and ornate rugs. She even noticed they had galleries with suits of armor! Still, the deal went ahead, but despite their best business efforts to make it work, it soon became obvious that trying to marry a four-year-old Internet-based company with a hundred-year-old, high-end auction house was just not going to work. Three years later, eBay pulled the plug and sold Butterfield & Butterfield to a British firm. Sometimes what seems like a good idea doesn't work in the real world and you have to admit your mistake, prune your portfolio, and move on.

Using This Anecdote

All too often, what makes sense in strict business terms doesn't make sense when corporate cultures clash. Not every acquisition works—in fact, statistically, more mergers fail than succeed—and sometimes the best thing to do is acknowledge the mistake and cut your losses now. Try this: "It's a shame it didn't work out with Company X, but we are far from alone. Meg Whitman tells the story of a company eBay bought that didn't quite fit into their portfolio . . ."

Source

Meg Whitman, *The Power of Many* (New York: Crown Publishers, 2010), pp. 193–195.

Meg Whitman

EBAY

Weighted Down

> "Feature Creep"
> Focus
> Tough Decisions

You can't please all of the people all of the time. As one of the pioneers—and survivors—in online business, eBay experienced what many competitors online faced, including something perhaps unique to high-tech ventures: "feature creep." It's the temptation to keep adding new bells and whistles to a basic system that already works well. While these changes are usually harmless, and often never fully used by all, if they accumulate, they start to make navigation online difficult, defeating the original purpose of making it easier for online users in the first place. Former eBay CEO Meg Whitman tells a story that around 2003, they began to notice their system was beginning to become overloaded—"feature creep" had set in. The decision was made to start pruning back some of the unnecessary features, but which ones? Each feature, while perhaps not always used by all users, had its own group of defenders, while the majority didn't care.

After careful consideration, the decision was made to drop the escrow feature, which was little understood and little utilized. There had also been a recent rise in escrow fraud, making the decision to discontinue the feature relatively easy. The next day, Whitman says, it seemed that every single fan of the escrow option wrote an email complaining about the move. Return emails were sent politely explaining the reasons behind the decision to eliminate the feature since so few people were using it and it was taking up space and using valuable resources that could be better deployed in the interest of the entire eBay community. While not everyone was happy with the decision, most were pleased to at least get a reply to their concerns. Still, a decision had to be made for the good of the entire site. "However good times may be," writes Whitman, "resources and time are always limited, and it is better to do three things well than ten things in a halfhearted way."

Using This Anecdote

Businesses may be able to build a better mousetrap, but they can also fall victim to overengineering it. Focus is critical when you have only so many resources and so much time at your disposal. Sometimes you have go back to basics. And while that may not please some individuals, you have to keep your eye on the bigger picture and make sure the business as a whole is not in jeopardy. Try this: "I know this was not an easy decision. I know some people are upset because we dropped X, but we have to keep the bigger picture in mind. Meg Whitman of eBay tells the story of . . ."

Source

Meg Whitman, *The Power of Many* (New York: Crown Publishers, 2010), pp. 196–199.

Meg Whitman

EBAY

"Hello, My Name Is . . ."

> Deflecting Insults
> Humor as a Weapon
> Sexism
> Taking the High Road
> Women Executives

Call it a terminal case of foot-in-mouth disease. Former eBay CEO Meg Whitman says that she often gets asked what it's like being a female executive in the male-dominated world of business and how she handles sexist attitudes. She says that she and other female execs feel they were lucky to have opportunities to prove themselves that previous generations of talented women did not. At the same time, there's a sense of having to prove one's competence, to show that one can be just as good—or better—than one's male counterparts. But not everyone has given up the old stereotypes. One of the lessons Whitman absorbed was Eleanor Roosevelt's observation that you can only feel inferior when you give someone else consent to put you down. Whitman's way of dealing with this type of confrontation is to use humor to parry and thrust against any attack.

She tells the story of attending a conference in 2000 that had brought together various political figures, CEOs, philanthropists, and other prominent individuals. Whitman had missed the opening night event but was able to start the conference by joining the second-day cocktail reception, during which spouses were also invited to attend. She didn't know anybody, so she went over to the first group of people she saw and introduced herself. One of the men in the group, a prominent California politician at the time, asked her, "And who are you married to?" The other men in the group winced at this person's obvious faux pas. Without missing a beat, Whitman said she was married to Griff Harsh, a neurosurgeon. The politician then smugly asked, "Since when do we invite doctors to this thing?" With the others desperately trying to signal the politician to stop, Whitman didn't hesitate, saying that her husband wasn't here, actually. "Oh, there's no reason you should have known," said Whitman. "I'm the president and CEO of eBay." Completely disarmed, the man went looking for the nearest rock to crawl under, dying of embarrassment. "As Mrs. Roosevelt said," says Whitman, "carry on in the face of an insult and you'll usually triumph."

Using This Anecdote

This is a great story for anyone—male or female—to demonstrate the dangers of stereotyping. It also delivers a great message that sometimes understated humor can do more to disarm others than outright confrontation. If others insist on taking the low road, rise above it. Try this: "We've all had our share of experiences where people tried to get the better of us. My advice is that despite the temptation to lash out, the best reaction is to calmly take the high road. I'm reminded of a story Meg Whitman of eBay told . . ."

Source

Meg Whitman, *The Power of Many* (New York: Crown Publishers, 2010), pp. 85–87.

Meg Whitman

EBAY

Three Thousand Miles for This?

> Board Meetings
> Corporate Culture
> Ignoring Advice
> "Old Boys" Attitude
> Soliciting Advice

Lead by example. But make sure the examples are *good* ones. Sometimes a CEO's personality can have a profound impact on the corporate culture of the company he or she leads. Meg Whitman writes that it's not unusual for the particular habits of the CEO to begin seeping into the DNA of the rest of the organization. If the CEO makes people wait, others below him or her will often do the same. If the CEO yells, others feel they have license to do the same, and so on. In 2001, Whitman agreed to serve on the board of a prominent New York financial services company. Board meetings were typically two-day affairs with the agenda handed out in advance so members had time to prepare.

Whitman tells the story of how she had read the materials thoroughly beforehand, writing out questions she had, etc. At the meeting, one item was slated to take up two hours. But the vast majority of time was spent presenting. With only five minutes left, Whitman got one question in, then the chairman moved on quickly to the next item on the agenda. Whitman was incensed at being given such short shrift. She stood up behind her chair and told him that she didn't appreciate putting in so much time analyzing the materials she had been given and then flying three thousand miles cross-country, only to be told that items on the agenda were FYI only—not for serious discussion. The embarrassed chairman then opened up the floor for more discussion, but by then it was clear to Whitman. Even though he had gone public and invited outsiders to serve on the company's board, its top-down culture had not changed. True decision making was apparently still being done in private. She lasted a few more meetings before pulling the plug on her board membership. "It was going to take a long time for this culture to change," she writes, "so I decided to move on."

Using This Anecdote

You can't just ask for people's opinions or input and then ignore them when they speak. This story shows some of the problems privately held companies have when making the transition to being publicly traded companies. Or that companies have when making major shifts in general. Corporate cultures rarely change overnight, and the CEO's stamp is often more powerful than people are willing to admit. Try this: "We're committed to an open dialogue here, not just running through a laundry list. I want *real* debate. I remember a story Meg Whitman once told . . ."

Source

Meg Whitman, *The Power of Many* (New York: Crown Publishers, 2010), pp. 89–91.

Jerry Yang

YAHOO!

When the Cat's Away

> Immigrant
> Meeting Demand
> Naming a Company
> Overcoming Odds

He's quite the immigrant success story. Jerry Yang, one of the founders of Yahoo!, was born in Taiwan. His father died when he was two years old and his mother moved the family to California when he was only nine. He had to learn a new language, but Jerry did so, and eventually earned himself bachelor's and master's degrees in electrical engineering at Stanford University. By the time he graduated, the economy was in a slowdown and there weren't many jobs in his field. He decided to enroll in a doctoral program at Stanford instead, in 1990.

Yang and another student, David Filo, were assigned to do research on computer-aided circuit design. At the time, however, their advisor was on sabbatical doing his own research. Bored and with not much to do, Yang started tooling around on a relatively new system called the "Internet." At the time, it was like having a telephone—but no phone book. Unless you knew others' addresses, this new technology wasn't particularly useful. Yang created his own page and started putting up links to favorite sites, including personal favorites, like sumo wrestling sites. That's how "Jerry and David's Guide to the World Wide Web" was born. Eventually the project got so big they decided to forgo their PhDs and start a search engine business instead. But they needed a name. Finally they decided on Yahoo!, which originated from two ideas. One was an inside joke among programmers. "Yet Another Compiler Complier" became "Yet Another Hierarchic Officious Oracle" or *Yahoo*. The word "yahoo" also came from Jonathan Swift's novel *Gulliver's Travels*, in which the "yahoos" were rude characters much in the same vein as the tech geeks of the day. Among other obvious qualities, Yang and Filo clearly had the ability to make fun of themselves.

Using This Anecdote

Yang's is a great success story to tell audiences. Call it fate—call it whatever you want—but it was also probably a good thing that Jerry Yang's doctoral advisor was off on sabbatical and the young entrepreneur had time to burn. Who knows if Yahoo! would have been created otherwise? Try this: "When it comes to creativity, some of the best ideas may stem from having too much time on one's hands. Consider the story of Jerry Yang . . ."

Source
Laura French, *Internet Pioneers: The Cyber Elite* (Berkeley Heights, NJ: Enslow Publishers Inc., 2001), pp. 85–88.

Mark Zuckerberg

FACEBOOK

The Final's When . . . ?

> Early Signs of Talent
> Information Sharing
> Playing to One's Strengths
> Quick Thinking

Facebook's phenomenal rise has been an incredible story in itself. One of Facebook's founders, Mark Zuckerberg, tells how he was still building the site a few weeks before finals. He was apparently significantly behind in one class in particular—art. Trying to balance the need to do well on his finals with the drive to get Facebook launched was proving too much. Realizing he was about to fail the art class unless he did something, Zuckerberg came up with an elegant solution.

A few days before the exam, he took all the images used in the class and created a website where people were encouraged to add their notes to a field beside the works of art discussed in class. The website was essentially a collective study tool. The benefit to Zuckerberg, of course, was the fact that others were filling in the notes he couldn't take because he was too busy setting up Facebook in his dorm room. But Zuckerberg apparently didn't benefit alone. He says the professor later said that class had received some of the best grades he had ever seen on any final he had given during his tenure at Harvard. Sharing information worked—and then some!

Using This Anecdote

One of the key attributes of the Internet is its ability to break down barriers to information—to "disintermediate" in tech jargon. If information is power, then power widely dispersed has benefits not just to the individual but to all users. This anecdote is also a good one for demonstrating quick thinking that plays to one's strengths in the face of pressure. In Zuckerberg's case, it was programming. Try this: "I know we're under a lot of pressure, but sometimes pressure breeds creative solutions that play to our strengths. We have the tools; we just have to realize it. There's a story about Mark Zuckerberg, the founder of Facebook . . ."

Source

Jason Kincaid, "Startup School: An Interview with Mark Zuckerberg," *TechCrunch*, October 24, 2009: http://techcrunch.com/2009/10/24/startup -school-an-interview-with-mark-zuckerberg.

Mark Zuckerberg

FACEBOOK

What's on Your Mind?

Good ideas need to work under the toughest conditions. Mark Zuckerberg says he and the group who launched Facebook followed a very simple philosophy: Do something people want, launch it early, and repeat. Started in his dorm room at Harvard, he says the immediate goal was not to make the venture as big as possible—in fact, it wasn't even a company until later—and to focus on adding value. After seeing the site's tremendous success at Harvard, where it went viral very quickly, Zuckerberg tells of how they tested the concept outside their own university.

Instead of trying it at schools that would have likely been eager to follow Harvard's lead, they decided to test the market by launching at universities Zuckerberg describes as "least receptive," including Yale, Columbia, and Stanford. When the concept eventually took off at these schools, they realized their original idea was not a one-shot wonder. As they say in show business, "It had legs." They had a winning formula on their hands, and it was worth putting more time and effort into the venture.

Using This Anecdote

There's a lesson in this story for everyone. While still in the testing phase, instead of trying out the concept where they knew it would likely be well received, Facebook's founders tried it where they knew it would be a hard sell. When it worked, it made it all the easier to sell the concept elsewhere. Try this: "I know we often say it makes sense to go after the low-hanging fruit first, but sometimes it makes sense to take the opposite approach when testing the viability of an idea. Take this example from Facebook . . ."

Source
Jason Kincaid, "Startup School: An Interview with Mark Zuckerberg," *TechCrunch*, October 24, 2009: http://techcrunch.com/2009/10/24/startup -school-an-interview-with-mark-zuckerberg.

Index

About the Author

Jim Holtje is currently the director of public affairs and speech-writer at a Fortune 500 company in New York City. He previously served as chief speechwriter to the president and CEO of Siemens USA, a $25 billion diversified company with more than sixty-two thousand employees throughout the United States. He also worked for three years as the English-language speechwriter to the president and CEO of Siemens AG, at the company's global headquarters in Munich, Germany. The editor of Prentice Hall's *Manager's Lifetime Guide to the Language of Power*, his prior book titles include *Divided It Stands: Can the United Nations Work?* for Turner Publishing of Atlanta as well as *201 Ways to Manage Your Time Better*, *201 Ways to Deal with Difficult People*, and *201 Ways to Say No Gracefully and Effectively* for McGraw-Hill. Holtje has worked at several public relations agencies and consultancies, servicing Fortune 500 companies including Chrysler, DaimlerChrysler, Deloitte Touche Tohmatsu, Deutsche Post, Eli Lilly, and Walmart. He holds a master's degree in international political economy from Columbia University's School of International and Public Affairs and a bachelor's degree from New York University's Washington Square and University College in political science and German. He lives with his wife in New York City.